THE
ENTREPRENEUR'S
GARDEN

THE NINE ESSENTIAL RELATIONSHIPS TO CULTIVATE YOUR WILDLY SUCCESSFUL BUSINESS

Divya Parekh

Copyright and Disclaimer

We support copyright of all intellectual property. Copyright protection continues to spark the seed of creativity in content producers, ensures that everyone has their voice heard through the power of words and the captivity of a story. Uniqueness of culture and content has been passed down through generations of writing and is the DNA of every intelligent species on our planet. This publication is intended to provide helpful and informative material. It is not intended to diagnose, treat, cure, or prevent any health problem or condition, nor is intended to replace the advice of a physician. No action should be taken solely on the contents of this book. Always consult your physician or qualified health-care professional on any matters regarding your health and before adopting any suggestions in this book or drawing inferences from it.

The author and publisher specifically disclaim all responsibility for any liability, loss or risk, personal or otherwise, which is incurred as a consequence, directly or indirectly, from the use or application of any contents of this book. Any and all product names referenced within this book are the trademark of their respective owners. None of these owners have sponsored, authorized, endorsed, or approved this book. Always read all information provided by the manufacturers' product labels before using their products. The author and publisher are not responsible for claims made by manufacturers.

Ordering Information:

Quantity Sales: Special discounts are available on quantity purchases by corporations, associations, and others. For details, contact the publisher at contact@divyaparekh.com

Printed in the United States of America
First Edition

THE IDEAL SPEAKER
FOR YOUR NEXT
EVENT!

Any organization that wants to invigorate, inspire and energize their team members to mobilize peak performance, then hire Divya for a keynote and/ or workshop training!!

To Contact or Book Divya to Speak:
The DP Group, LLC
150 Wrenn Drive, Unit #584
Cary, NC 27512
(888) 631-8611

contact@divyaparekh.com
www.divyaparekh.com/speaking
https://www.facebook.com/beyondconfidenceforsuccess/
https://twitter.com/coachdivya/

Advance Praise for *The Entrepreneur's Garden*

"This is a practical, helpful and inspiring book for anyone who dreams of being successful in their own business."
Brian Tracy – Author – Million Dollar Habits

"When you read Divya's book, you will discover new methods for building your business while re-remembering potent wisdom tips you once knew and forgot. Divya combines storytelling with facts in such a manner that you quickly turn pages to find the next tool which will take your business over the top."
Coach Winn, Two-time Olympian, Originator of the WIN Philosophy, Founder of CoachWinnSpeaks.com

"If you want to experience more success in personal life and business, then follow and use the strategies by my friend Divya! They will help you to achieve greater success and live a more abundant life!"
James Malinchak, Featured on ABCs Hit TV Show, "Secret Millionaire" "The World's #1 Big Money Speaker® Trainer & Coach!" Founder, www.BigMoneySpeaker.com

"There is NOTHING more critical to the success of your business than RELATIONSHIPS. Cultivating long-term strategic relationships is arguably the most important marketing activity you can invest your time in. Divya's book will give you a complete strategy to implement, and the firepower you need to build lasting relationships with the kind of people that can change your business and life forever."
Josh Turner Founder - Linked Selling

"Imagine Patrick Lencioni, Steven Covey and Thich Nhat Hanh co-wrote a book on being an entrepreneur – now you have some idea of how this unique book reads. Following Sally on her journey through developing the nine vital relationships for the success of her business, you learn all she learns from her mentor Dee, and get to apply all the tools to your own entrepreneurial journey. Divya Parekh has written a success manual like none I have ever read – I wish I could write like this."

Deiric McCann
Executive Vice President - International
Profiles International Inc. (Division of Wiley & Sons)

Divya does a wonderful job easing the stress of being an entrepreneur. Her spot-on, simple steps makes it easy to follow and apply. The book is written in a narrative form, so the reader becomes engaged in the characters, while learning important guidance at the same time. If one applies Dee's wisdom and suggestions as Sally does, they will be able to move their business forward. Entrepreneurship is not for the weak at heart, but Divya's book can provide the necessary roadmap for a successful business.

Rhonda York, MS-Executive Coaching, PCC, BCC
President/Chief Executive Coach, Team Wide Solutions, LLC;
Conversational Intelligence Certified Coach

This book has such a wow factor on so many levels: the story between Sally and Dee is masterful, the clarity of the message for each relationship level, and the action items suggested are spot-on. Whether you are a new entrepreneur or a seasoned one, I guarantee you will value Divya Parekh's perspective on mastering the art of the nine key relationship to apply to your business. Take time to read and absorb this book.

Lauren Midgley,
Time Behaviorist, Author and Business Strategist
www.LaurenMidgley.com

From a familiar beginning for entrepreneurs the author walks the reader through an in-depth process starting with understanding him or herself, then examining nine relationships to facets of business success. The book covers the most important relationships in business:

- Time
- Money
- Market
- Team
- Partners
- Death
- Legacy
- Results

As a successful university associate professor, scientist, biotechnology professional, global business relationship and leadership coach and consultant, Divya Parekh has vast experience that she draws from and shares in this book.

Through exercises at the conclusion of chapters, readers can discover practical answers to improving their businesses. This insightful and practical book has been beneficial to me and can help other entrepreneurs improve their businesses and save time to spend in their personal lives.

Drew Becker
Publisher Realization Press

"Like her character Dee, Divya offers entrepreneurs thought and development provoking questions and warm wisdom. You will be inspired and equipped with the tools to confidently transform yourself and your business to a level of success and happiness, in service to others that will stretch your imagination."

Marilyn O'Hearne, MA, Culturally Intelligent Master Certified
Coach Sharing Power, Building Trust, Promoting Peace

Real motivation for today's entrepreneur. Divya relates as only a true entrepreneur can. I can easily see myself in Sally's shoes, working so hard at times but not seeing the growth I want in my business, all the while losing the enthusiasm that first drove me when I started. The relationships Divya speaks of in her book I believe are the keys to running a successful business. It makes complete sense that improving these individual relationships will have a huge impact on us personally as well as professionally. I love the fact that Divya not only shares the relationship secrets with us, she goes into great detail on each one, picking it apart until all aspects of the relationship are revealed. The details are followed up by in-depth questions, making you really think about what it is you want, what you're doing, and what you need to do differently. The book is easy to read, not your usual "how to" manual. It spells out all you need to do in order to be successful, without being dry and dull. This is the book that can raise you from a stagnant entrepreneur to a passionate and successful business owner.

Shannon M. Jenke
Financial Advisor
The Leith Jenke Group
Private Wealth Management

I loved the way Divya shared the 9 relationships you need to understand and implement to reach your ultimate entrepreneurial success. By weaving the content and lessons through a relatable characters, and offering explanations that made it easy to follow, I could see myself in "Sally." By building that connection with the character and seeing similarities in my business growth, I believe that helped bring home some very important steps that I need to take as an entrepreneur. This book will help you build, and link the relationships that you need, to achieve what every entrepreneur wants - a life that allows you to make a difference in the world, have a successful business, and also keep work-life balance.

Tracey Ehman
Online Presence & Social Media Strategist

Divya Parekh has captured the core business success elements and wrapped it up in a delightful story. The practical sections of each chapter allow the reader to grow alongside the main character. Reading this book is like going on the journey to success with a mentor in your pocket.

Laura Rubinstein, Social Media & Marketing Strategist, Bestselling Author "Social Media Myths Busted: The Small Business Guide To Online Revenue"

In a world consumed by metrics, The Entrepreneur's Garden embraces how a business or organization leader needs to work with people if they ever hope to realize their dreams. The day after I finished the book, I had an opportunity to work with a nonprofit and drew on the principles of the nine relationships to help that executive director have a clear understanding of how to get her ship back on course. The narrative is unique and enjoyable to read while the lessons are invaluable for business and life.

JJ McKeever, CEO - JJ Writing-Consulting

The Entrepreneur's Garden by Divya Parekh is on point. This book clearly illustrates the problems many entrepreneurs often face when they begin to grow. It not only states the challenges but also provides a plain and simple guide to how to navigate through them.

It all starts with your relationship with yourself to include your values. Once you clearly understand your values you can align those with your decisions and actions, which will lead you onto your path of purpose and destiny.

She also explains authenticity in all facets of your life, which creates trust and connections. This is important because in order for sustainable growth and service to others, you must know when to delegate and when to ask for help.

Ultimately you learn to protect your time and space by staying true to self, which creates trust, a necessary ingredient for healthy sustainable relationships to develop and be maintained.

Healthy relationships with yourself and other facets of life is critical to your success in business and personal development.

You will then be able to live your legacy through service to others and collaboration.

If you are a budding entrepreneur or established entrepreneur, this book is a must read. Share with your network.

Dr. Jamila Battle, MD
BestSelling Author: From Abuse to Abundance"

Divya is out to help people get better at what they are trying to create in their life and business. And she is totally committed to the journey. She is extremely adept at co-creating with you business strategies that work. This is one of her great strengths, along with her evidence-based coaching approach, and she gets results.

Leon Vanderpol
Founder, CenterforTransformationalCoaching.com, Professional
Coach Training & Mentoring

Throughout the past 20 years, I have read hundreds of books, taken many courses, and completed over a dozen self-help programs. All of this was an effort to fix what I thought was a lack vision and self-discipline. Although I have grown and prospered from investing in these programs, none have had the affect and results of The Entrepreneur's Garden, by Divya Parekh.

My Ah-Ha moment came as a result of reading the conversations within the story between the characters, Dee and Sally. They led me to look at how my life lined up with my values, vision, and mission, where I found that I have, in fact, been self-disciplined. All this time I had been kicking myself for lacking the will to have, do, and be more – when all along I just needed to choose whether to live with my current values or reset with new ones. Now I know that once that is done, I have the perfect guidebook for taking the next steps: The Entrepreneur's Garden.

Thank you Divya!

Nancy Thyme
Business Consultant

FOREWORD

Since creating the Keller Influence Indicator® (KII®) Assessment, I have met thousands of people interested in and using our measurement of Influence Potential. However, there was an individual who stood head and shoulders above the crowd and excelled in her application and results of influencing potential. Her name is Divya Parekh.

When I founded and became CEO of KKI, Inc., I knew the tides were changing around how organizations did business. It was no longer only a product and service destination as much as it was becoming a people and purpose destination. That is when I introduced the idea of Being Influential to the world. How Being Influential is a higher order of influence.

Being Influential requires an individual to connect with the traits that determine how well they will impact another human being. How they will add value, build trust, and how people embrace one another. Again, in a word, relationship.

Divya Parekh has written a highly engaging book that leads the reader through the journey of the nine most important relationships in the life of an entrepreneur. Each relationship is described along with exercises on how to build that relationship to be healthy. Divya accomplishes this in a way that is timely, relevant, and actionable.

This book is *timely*. Having entered into the world of global relationships, organizations have now found themselves in need of deeper, more trusting and better developed relationships, at all levels within their organizations. Entrepreneurs are at the pinnacle of building their business from the strength of relationship both with internal and external customers.

Second, this book is *relevant*. I believe that entrepreneurs are seeking to find how to remove the potential barriers, which can often times be themselves, in order to reach not only success, but sustainable success. Entrepreneurs find themselves in a constant struggle of defining and understanding their relationship to the many factors that constitute the founding of fulfilling businesses.

The entrepreneur has to take great care with the emotional connection they bring to their business. Building a business is more than bricks and mortar. To the entrepreneur, it is the expression of their creativity and strong desire to offer their gifts to the world. Without that emotional connection and freedom of expression, entrepreneurs cannot reach their full potential.

Finally, this book is *actionable*. Entrepreneurs today need to see themselves as the bedrock of the future. They need to keep their minds engaged but not at the expense of their hearts. That is what successful entrepreneurs know and practice. That is one of the things the *Entrepreneur's Garden* does so well – it gives us practical, specific actions we can take to avoid the traps and "time-wastes" of being an entrepreneur. Each of the nine relationships concludes with exercises and a step-by-step process for developing that relationship. For example, one of the nine entrepreneur relationships is to "Manage Your Brand . . . to build a healthy relationship." This is about reputation. Paying attention to how I reveal myself to the world with integrity and honesty is one of the most valuable lessons I learned from my parents. Knowing the importance of something so simple is a foundational piece to every relationship.

The *Entrepreneur's Garden* is a transformational book that quickly and thoroughly shows what exists behind the curtain of sustainable relationships, which are critical for entrepreneurial success. It eloquently addresses the entrepreneur's makeup and relationship to core values to money to networking to legacy, just to name a few.

In the *Entrepreneur's Garden*, Divya expertly uses the art of story to take the reader on the journey to discover nine relationships that are important in the entrepreneur's life, not only becoming a business success, but doing so without insurmountable sacrifice.

Divya has great knowledge and understanding of the entrepreneurial mindset. What makes it tick, how it makes decisions, and the never-ending cycle of thinking about business. She has successfully shed light on the endless confusion surrounding the role and purpose of relationship in everything the entrepreneur does, personally and professionally.

Karen Keller, Ph.D.
Founder & CEO, KKI, Inc.
Creator of *Keller Influence Indicator*® *(KII*®*)*

ABOUT DIVYA PAREKH

Divya Parekh is an in-demand motivational speaker, a leading business relationship and leadership coach, and an Amazon best seller. Divya has guided many entrepreneurs, CEOs, and management personnel into realizing their goals and reaching their next level of accomplishment. She accomplishes this through her individual coaching sessions, leadership talks, and workshops. Divya's best-selling books, including her newest, The Entrepreneur's Garden – Nine Essential Relationships to Cultivate a Wildly Successful Business, serve as the foundation for many leaders in business and other organizations. Her other books include Stress Management, Mindfulness Mastery, Critical Thinking, Candid Critique, Appreciative Inquiry, Leadership and Influence, and Emotional Intelligence. She also co-authored the international best-selling book, The Voyage to Your Vision.

First and foremost, Divya Parekh values people, and it is her connection with clients and audiences that make her so effective. She communicates well with everyone and brings her 25+ years of experience in academia and the entrepreneur world into her teaching. This wealth of knowledge combines with her formal training in mentoring and coaching to have individuals, companies, and organizations seeking her out for her knowledge and expertise.

Divya works on the international level with leaders, achievers, and entrepreneurs. She believes the key factor in success on any level is the partnerships we cultivate. For her, the relationship is king. She helps others to learn the exponential power in developing a thorough understanding of your business partners and giving of yourself. She provides her services to the academia, corporate, and entrepreneurial worlds on how to seed, grow and sustain productive relationships.

Her compelling interactive presentations, talks, and workshops are always well received and given high marks of success and acclaim. If you are looking for knowledge and inspiration to help you or your organization move forward in our highly competitive and fast changing world, go to her website for more details and contact information:

www.divyaparekh.com
contact@divyaparekh.com

PREFACE

The Entrepreneur's Garden reveals business methods and techniques through the Nine Essential Relationships needed for success in life and business. As a global business relationship and leadership coach, I have developed and refined these principles over time, and have seen many of my clients reap the fruits of its results.

As I was reflecting on different ways to present these concepts in a book, I began to research how people best learn. The results were clear. People of all ages seem to learn and relate best with stories involving characters illustrating their life experiences.

Once I decided on the style of the book, I began tracking the impact of the Nine Essential Relationships in people's interactions and outcomes. These records became a series of conversations and interactions between Dee (the coach) and Sally (the entrepreneur). Creating characters that a reader could relate to fulfilled my quest to construct an engaging book detailing the methods and impact of the nine relationships.

The lessons in this book can help any entrepreneur's garden thrive. Passion for what you do is the driving force for anyone setting up their own business. The problem is that the passion can be worn down by the very real headaches and complexity of developing and growing your company. It doesn't have to be that way!

TABLE OF CONTENTS

1. Introduction to Relationship Matrix: Identify the challenges and pain points that most entrepreneurs encounter. -------------------------------- 21
- ○ Five questions to ponder 28
- ○ How to make the most out of this book...30

2. Live the Life You Want: Relationship with Self is the authenticity that comes from knowing and understanding your purpose and values------ 32
- ○ The Power of Values as Life Compass 35
- ○ Co-relation of Self-Relationship and Business Success...................37
- ○ Understanding the How Model 38
- ○ Mindfulness 41
- ○ Authenticity 41
- ○ Summation...42
- ○ Defining Your Values Exercise:..42
- ○ Enneagon Business Success Tool 43

3. Time is the Currency of Life: Relationship with Time rides on your values, vision, and mission. Time is the world's most valuable commodity and will enrich your life. -- 45
- ○ Thinking Questions..46
- ○ How to Strengthen Your Time Relationship....................................50
- ○ Prioritization Matrix 52
- ○ Visioning Exercise...53
- ○ Effective Planning – Mission...54
- ○ Efficient Execution 55
- ○ Summation – Impact to Business 55
- ○ Action Exercise..55

4. The Money Conundrum: Relationship with Money - Developing a
Money Mindset -- 57

  ◦ Thinking Questions 57
  ◦ What is the Relationship to Money................................60
  ◦ Why the Relationship with Money Is Important............62
  ◦ How Do You Achieve Your Relationship with Money 63
  ◦ Creating the Money Mindset 65
  ◦ Business Plan Elements..66
  ◦ Process for Creating a Money Management Discipline 67
  ◦ Business Summation 68
  ◦ Money Action Exercise 68

5. Interlude & Networking: A primer on the value of networking and
tips to rock it! --- 70

6. Knowing Your Market: Relationship with Market enables you to know
and understand your ideal client, establish your brand, make a positive
impact, and serve your clients -- 97

  ◦ Define Your Ideal Client 102
  ◦ Branding and You 104
  ◦ Defining Your Brand 105
  ◦ Develop Your Brand..105
  ◦ Delivering the Promise 106
  ◦ Summation – Impact to Business 106
  ◦ Exercise to Manage Your Brand 108

7. The Power of Teamwork: Relationship to Team covers the creation
of your team. It includes organizational planning, hiring, and training
employees and contract workers. --------------------------------------111

  ◦ The Relationship with Team..112
  ◦ Questions for Team Leader 113
  ◦ Why Team Is Important to Business....................................115
  ◦ Processes and Systems..118
  ◦ Hiring the Right People 118
  ◦ Bringing out the Best 119
  ◦ Various Phases of Teams 120
  ◦ Setting Objectives and Goals 120

- Crafting the Team Success Principles and Action Plan:.............. 121
- Summation – Impact to Business 124
- Exercise from a Team Member's Perspective:.............................. 125

8. **Purposeful Partners:** Relationship with Partners helps you identify, enroll, and build relationships with a wide spectrum of people where all benefit from the partnership. --131
- What is Relationship with Partners.. 131
- Why Every Aspect of the Partnership is Important to Business 132
- Processes and Systems... 135
- Determining the Right Partner.. 136
- Bringing out the Best... 137
- Commitment to Collaboration 138
- Various Phases of Partnership 138
- Setting Goals 139
- Institute your partner-specific "success principles" for planning execution 139
- Summation – Impact to Business 141
- Purposeful Partnership Pulse Check Action Exercise.................. 143

9. **The Death of Fear:** Relationship with Death brings peace of mind. It focuses on your "Why." It also reiterates your values, vision, and your mission as you learn to transcend beyond consciousness to experience timelessness. ---144
- What is Relationship with Death 147
- Why Relationship with Death is Important to Business 147
- How to Strengthen Your Relationship with Death....................... 150
- Scanning the Future 151
- Achieving Heart and Mind Harmony 152
- Achieving Business Harmony.. 154
- Summation – Impact to Business 156
- Success Pyramid Exercise... 157

10. **Living Your Legacy:** Relationship with Legacy captures the power of living a legacy through your business. In this chapter, the reader learns how to expand your gifts in a way that neighbors, the community, and the world may benefit, whether you live it now or you leave it upon your exit from this world. ---158

○   What is Relationship with Legacy 161

○   Good or Bad, Everyone Leaves a Legacy 161

○   Why is Relationship with Legacy Important to Business 162

○   How Can You Strengthen the Relationship with Legacy 163

○   Legacy through Wealth 164

○   Legacy through Heart and Mind Share 164

○   Legacy in Daily Life and Business 164

○   Legacy through Dedicated Time and Talent 166

○   Summation – Impact to Business 166

○   Legacy Action Exercise 167

11. The Results of Success: Relationship with results is how you measure success, clearly define the outcomes, and determining the progress as you work towards your goals. --169

○   What is Relationship with Results 172

○   Why Relationship with Results is Important to Business 172

○   How to Strengthen the Relationship with Results 173

○   First essential of sustained success – Know the Forest, Know the Trees 173

○   Second essential of sustained success – Continuous Growth and Evolution 174

○   Student Leader for Life – Own Your Learning, Unlearning, and Relearning 174

○   30,000 Feet Business Overview 175

○   Continuous Growth and Evaluation 176

○   Summation – Impact to Business 178

○   Results Action Exercise 179

○   Epilogue 182

INTRODUCTION TO RELATIONSHIP MATRIX

Twenty years from now, you will be more disappointed by the things you didn't do than by the ones you did do. So throw off the bowlines. Sail away from the safe harbor. Catch the trade winds in your sails. Explore. Dream. Discover.

-Mark Twain

"Ugh. Entrepreneurship isn't all it is cracked up to be. Owning my personal business is *hard*," I said to my windshield.

I do not often talk to myself, but this was a tough day. I had been in my car all day driving from office to office. I was meeting and networking with people to grow my business. I was making decent money after setting up my company a couple of years ago, however, it was nowhere near what I want to make. My operating costs were high and I wasn't making enough to hire help or outsource some of the work. While I thought I knew how to run my executive coaching business, I was learning the hard way that I didn't know what was involved in business operations.

My name is Sally. I have made significant progress from those days when I was totally consumed with my business, and driven to the point of talking to my windshield. It wasn't my style to be a workaholic, but it became my day to day survival. Looking back on that stressful day, I see now that it was the beginning of a new path in my business career. I was going to meet a couple of old friends that night, hoping to remind myself to take a break and go out for some fun. I couldn't even remember the last time I had a night out.

I pulled into the parking lot of Ma Paizen Restaurant, which has a beautiful view overlooking the ocean. Waiting for Mikayla and Lynn, who were friends from college, I relaxed in my car and reflected how easy college had been for me. I had a job lined up before graduation day and started working right away. Although I liked it, I wanted more control over my life. There was certainly security in the job I had, but I didn't see any clear path for promotion in the near future. I recognized that the corporate world had worked for my parents. They were both with the same companies for over twenty years. I thought I wanted that too, but after working for a while, I realized that I needed more challenges. I also wanted to control my schedule instead of it controlling me. That was when I decided that starting my own business was the way to go.

I'm not sure if it was the lack of a mentor or experience, but my little company came to control me, not the other way around. My daily mantra became, "If only something would just fall into place." That particular day had been typical, ending with a tension-filled meeting. My client and his consulting company could not agree on how to move forward on a project. I would have been more productive banging my head against the wall! With the pressure on my fried brain, I got on the phone and insisted that Mikayla, Lynn, and I get together.

I smiled as I saw them pull in. They made it! As they leaped out of the car, we embraced in one giant group hug. It had been far too long since we caught up with one another. After ordering, we chatted and laughed as we talked about our lives. It had been months since we had been together and there was a lot to discuss. After a few minutes, I realized that the only thing we were talking about was work. There was no talk of other friends, potential relationships, family happenings...nothing like that. That was my wake-up call when I began to realize what had happened. Our businesses controlled us.

Having so much in common, the three of us had become great friends in college. That relationship extended into our careers. Not breaking the cycle of commonality, we all leaped into the murky world of owning our own business. I became an executive coach/consultant, Mikayla - an image consultant, and Lynn - an event planner. Each of us had left decent full-time jobs to strike out on our own. While we were establishing good reputations in our particular lines of work, our businesses had stalled. As we talked, I saw that my friends shared my frustration of wanting to grow, but knowing that things were not going smoothly or quickly.

Lynn said, "I had so much enthusiasm when I started out, but after running the business for a while, it has become difficult to keep up that same level of passion. Sometimes I feel my enthusiasm is dying because I have been working so hard at times."

"I know what you mean," said Mikayla. "I'd bust my chops responding to my clients. The word of mouth generated more business than I was able to handle. However, having more clients means that I have even more to do, and I am already functioning on overload. I have been wearing so many hats that things have started to slip. If they invent a 35-hour day, I'll be working 30 of them

"We certainly sound like we are in the same boat," I said. "What changed for us?"

The ensuing discussion was interesting. We liked owning our businesses, and we enjoyed the services we provided. However, none of us had cracked the secret of how to grow our companies. We realized that if we didn't change our entrepreneurial strategies, we would not have a life outside of it.

Lynn summed it up when she said, "It's a paradox. We want our companies to thrive. The bigger we become, the more we enhance our reputation, which brings us new clientele. However, we put more work on ourselves with more clients."

"Maybe," Mikayla wistfully answered, "having that bigger business might help enliven our passion. I know more income and connections would make me happier. At least, I think so. More money would mean that I could outsource the work I do not like to do. I'd rather give the job to someone who is good at it. Then I would have more freedom to be more creative and do what I love to do."

"That's great, guys, but how do we bring in more clients and make more connections?" I inquired. "Let's come up with some ideas. I'm all for ramping up my enthusiasm again."

After a brainstorming session over tiramisu, we decided that each of us would try a different way to grow our business. Then we would meet up again in a few months and compare how we did. I hoped that our growth would jump-start our passion and give our collective enthusiasm a much-needed boost.

I woke up the next morning with renewed fire. Even though it was the weekend, I experienced a certainty that my dream of being a successful entrepreneur was going to happen. Maybe the long days and risk taking would be worth it after all. As I was making coffee, it struck me. "You know what would be great?" I said to my kitchen. "If I find a mentor to help me in this journey, I can learn from his or her experience."

I continued to ponder on this idea. As a coach, I knew the value I provided to my clients was guiding them through their difficulties. There is value going to someone who can see what you are experiencing objectively. All the better if that person was successful in dealing with the issues I was facing. I needed a successful business owner who wasn't afraid to share their formula for success.

Obviously, Mikayla, Lynn, and I are not doing the right things to take our business to the next level and retain our passion, joy, and creativity. Maybe with a mentor, we could learn the ropes and become better entrepreneurs, get our joy back, and not feel so lost. I laughed to myself. "Where on earth would we find someone like that?" I spent the day trolling the internet looking for someone or something that would be a help. There were many choices, but none hit the right chord.

My good mood faded as I puzzled more over my problem. Doubt crept in around the edges of my mind. What if my business failed? I didn't want to go back to working for someone else. However, the way I was working now, I did not have free personal time. Was I even meant for business?

I didn't want to spend my entire Saturday inside with my brain flat lining, so I headed out. It was a beautiful day, and I walked toward the beach. A quick stroll on the sand would be invigorating. Feeling the water lapping over my feet always relaxed me as much as a massage. Maybe if I calmed my mind, inspiration would hit me.

It did…sort of. It came in the form of a thick, blond golden retriever. He ran toward me at full speed. I braced myself, but instead of leaping at me, he put on the brakes and ran around me in circles, playfully barking. He seemed so happy that I laughed. That's when I realized there was a party up ahead. That must have been from where the dog came.

I heard music and realized that somebody was strumming a guitar. Laughter spread across the beach from the group. People played Frisbee and roasted marshmallows over a fire pit. The retriever, who I later found was named Buddy, herded me to the party. As I slowly approached, I noticed something…or rather someone…who was the center of attention. She was in the middle of this joy and mirth. She was an older woman sitting in a beach chair sipping what appeared to be a mojito.

"Hi, I'm Dee. And you are…?" the woman inquired.

The question startled me. I didn't think Dee had even seen me yet. "I'm…um…Sally," I replied, surprised at her straightforwardness.

"Well, it's lovely to meet you, Sally. Have some food. There's plenty to go around," Dee instructed, gesturing toward a table of snacks.

"Thanks so much, but I probably shouldn't. I'm watching my weight."

"Oh, come now! Life is for *living*," Dee giggled. "I'm in my eighties and have never been better!"

Now I was truly surprised. This woman barely looked a day over 60, and a youthful 60 at that. "So what's the party for?" I asked.

"Oh! This shindig?" Dee replied. "It's my 84th birthday party, dear."

Looking at the numerous people in attendance, I decided to inquire further. As I sat down beside Dee, I asked, "Are they your family? All these people?"

"Well, yes, in a way!" Dee smiled. "I've been a relationship entrepreneur most of my life. Many of these people have been in my community for years. We celebrate one another, allow each person to be themselves, and are always there for one another. Some may be clients, friends or colleagues. So yes, they are my family by choice. We've become quite close over the years."

Dee continued. "People's love and friendship have nurtured and enriched my life. It gives new meaning to entrepreneurship when clients become lifelong friends and collaborators, rooting for each other. You want to see each other succeed. For me, it has always been about living a legacy rather than just leaving one."

"So…you're not leaving a legacy?" I asked.

While I tried to get a feeling for this unique, beautiful woman I just met, a tall redhead holding a s'more in each hand approached. "One for me and one for you," chirped the woman as she gave a s'more to Dee.

Before devouring the treat, Dee turned to me and explained, "Oh, but I am leaving a legacy! It lives in each individual here, including you." I get a strong feeling that you are a business owner."

"But you just met me," I said, feeling more than a little puzzled that she had me figured out. "Yes, I am a business owner." Obviously you have been very successful in business. How did you ever make it as an entrepreneur?"

"By building relationships," Dee replied in a very poised manner. "It's all about making connections and helping others. I often think about it as cultivating a beautiful garden. To me, that means growing a variety of healthy plants. They are all different, but with care, they live and thrive together," she finished.

I stayed into the evening. This woman captivated me. The camaraderie of the group never let up. They were very friendly, and I got to know some of them. They were all connected to Dee in some fashion, and they told me stories of how she had helped them at some point. Whether they were involved in one of her companies, a client, or even a rival, they all had a story of how they had learned from her and each other. I wanted to hear more stories as the sun dipped beneath the darkening waves. Guitar melodies continued to fill the air, and the bonfire grew taller and taller.

At one point, I found myself standing next to Dee watching a man and woman sing an Irish song to the guitar player's music. As I listened, I felt amazement that last night, my friends and I felt lackluster trying to determine out where to turn for help and today, I walked into exactly what I needed. I met an obviously successful entrepreneur with a life. She relaxed with a score of people whom she had met in her endeavors. This is what I wanted my life to be!

I looked at Dee, took a deep breath, and blurted out, "I would be honored to have you as my mentor. You are unlike anyone I have ever met. A couple of friends and I were talking last night how we are at a crucial stage with our businesses. We want to grow but can't figure out how to do it without killing ourselves. If you were willing to share your ideas, I would love to bring your secrets together in a book. Do you know how many people would benefit from learning what you know about entrepreneurship?"

Dee grinned from ear to ear. Thrusting her arm towards the crowd, she said, "I probably did that for some of these folks. I never believed there was any reason to keep success a secret. I know the benefits of giving back to others whenever you have a chance. I am fascinated with the idea of a book. I have often thought of it, but that's one thing I never got around to doing. There is one condition, though."

I was worried about what the catch was going to be. Dee quickly dispelled any fears that leaped to my mind. She said, "Sally, you have to learn, grow, and implement actions as we go through the process and grow your business as well. What do you say?"

"Wow!" "I'm in!" I exclaimed. "When do we get started?"

Dee chuckled at my enthusiasm and said, "I walk every day on the beach around six o'clock in the morning. I enjoy the morning and start by meditating with the waves. Why don't you join me? You'll become familiar with my routine."

As I enthusiastically told her I would be there, Dee held up her hand. "Oh, yes, one more thing. Between our sessions, I will give you some questions that you need to ask yourself. It will stretch you to think wisely about who you are and where you want to be. I think of them as growth questions."

"I have no problem with that," I told her. "I think one of my problems lately is that I have been so busy "doing" my business, I don't seem to have time to do any thinking."

"That can happen when we get caught up in our businesses," said Dee, "but without processing our actions and plans, they won't improve."

"I am so happy you are going to mentor me. Is there any key to what we will be discussing?"

Dee thought for a few seconds and said, "As I mentioned, it all comes down to relationships." She held up her hand as I was about to hit her with another question. "There are nine key relationships that will bring you success as an entrepreneur. However, you will have to be patient because it is strategic to explore each one of them at a time and then understanding the dynamics between them. Which is exactly what we will do."

"I know. I'm excited; that's all. Is there anything that I should be aware of before we get started?"

She said, "Come with me." She led me over to the makeshift bar that was set up. Buddy followed us and he rested his head on my thigh as we sat on stools. Dee took a cocktail napkin and asked the bartender for a pen. She took a few minutes to scribble some things down. Handing me the napkin, she said, "Far be it from me to curb anyone's enthusiasm. There are a few questions for you to ponder tonight. The questions will help you think in the right direction. Read them when you get home."

I put the napkin in my back pocket. We stood up, and Dee gave me a hug. "I will look for you on the beach. Join me when you can."

Whatever dark mood was trying to take me down earlier in the day was completely gone. I found myself skipping and humming as I headed back up the beach toward my car. Driving home, I tried to identify the mood I was in. As I reached my condo, it dawned on me. I was feeling hope!

I was home for three minutes before I took out Dee's note and read it. There were five questions on the napkin.

1. What are your challenges and pain problems?

This was easy. I feel helpless in successfully expanding my business. Sometimes, I feel overwhelmed, frustrated, stressed, and seem to have lost the passion for my business.

2. Does it matter that you resolve your challenges and pain points. Why?

Yes, it matters a great deal! I wanted to feel joy and challenged with my business, not cranky and exhausted. I love the creative side of what I do. I want to devote more time to writing blogs, designing logos for my business, and preparing inspiring speeches. I enjoy devising plans for clients to solve their problems and help them find their "Ah-hah!" moments on their way to success. I want to achieve my true business, career, and life goals.

3. What will your life look like in five years if you do not do anything about your problems?

I thought about the people I have coached, and the effect it would have on them and others if I did nothing about the problem. I visualized my family and friends who had stood beside me in the startup phase, and how it would affect them if my business didn't survive. My life would look unfulfilled, and I would be carrying the heavy burden of knowing that I was letting down others, as well as myself. I may be working in the corporate world again in 5 years if I did nothing about the problem. I would look about 80 years old before I'm 40. Worse, I would feel that way. I want to be young, even like Dee at some point, but it was never going to happen at the rate I was going.

4. What will your life look like if you resolved your problems?

My life would be a picture of confidence, knowing that I was able to face problems and implement the solutions. I would be able to make decisions and take actions to create opportunities where none existed. I would once again feel confident, joyful, and at peace with myself. I would be helping people, as I always wanted to do. The wealth, success and quality lifestyle I desired would be possible. I would assemble a team aligned with my vision. If I do that, anything would be possible.

5. What can you do to resolve your situation?

This question will take time to answer as I explore, learn and integrate the nine relationships in my life that Dee mentioned. Twenty-four hours ago, making my dreams a reality, was a hopeless vision. After meeting Dee, I felt like I found the key to open the locked door I kept banging my head against. I talked to enough people tonight to figure out that this woman had talent, knowledge, and experience that I wanted to tap. I felt honored that she jumped at my idea.

I don't know what made me suggest the book idea to her. I love to write and create, but as I got ready for bed, I realized that it came down to my desire to help others. I know that Lynn, Mikayla, and I were a drop in a sea of entrepreneurs who are searching for success. When my experiences with Dee helped others, I knew I would be sharing the legacy.

I challenge the reader exactly how Dee tested me the first night that we met. This story is very real, and as you read along, I challenge you, "to learn, grow, and implement actions as we go through the process and grow your business as well." You will see how the fruits of your garden can multiply as you replace the weeds of doubt, procrastination, fear and apathy with the healthy seeds of the Nine Essential Relationships.

HOW TO MAKE THE MOST OF THIS BOOK

1. Read the chapter with a pencil and different colored highlighters to highlight key points that resonate with you. Make notes in a separate journal or in the book itself.

2. If you do not like the book to be cluttered, buy different colored sticky notes. Use green ones to represent that you are ready to take action, or you have been taking actions, yellow represents that you have been hesitating to take action and need to think about it, and red or dark pink represents that you are stuck on something. Write down how you will move forward on it.

3. If need be, read the chapter again. Reading and re-reading the book is similar to peeling onions. Give yourself time to reflect and realize your areas of potential. If you find resistance to changing, ask yourself why you are resisting. Would change benefit me?

4. Think about connections and conflicts with your existing thoughts and create a plan as to how you will tackle a different one each week.

5. Write out the actions on an index card and place it where you can see and it reminds you daily.

Above all, remember, it took years to get to where you are. It will take you some time to develop new habits.

Keep Track of Your Progress (monitor these with regards to personal and business development):

1. As you advance into mastery of each relationship, you will continue to gather reflections and insights into improving actions that increase your personal abilities in practicing mindfulness and interacting consistently.

2. You will find that developing new behaviors and having new perspectives will increase your ability to learn and grow by leaps and bounds.

3. You will find yourself energized and ready to take on challenges and make the most of the opportunities.

4. You will see results in a business where people are responding to you at an entirely another level. Doors will open that you never expected:

   a. You will be more confident and not shy about sharing the transformation your products and services provide your clients since you are changing their lives.

   b. Your emotional and financial freedom will grow.

   c. You will find that you can manage risk with courage and creativity.

   d. Meeting your goals will become manageable.

   e. Your business will expand.

   f. You discover your work is making a positive impact, and you are inspiring others with your leadership example.

CHAPTER 2
LIVE THE LIFE YOU WANT

Grateful I am,
For who I am.
Today, I am,
Ready to take on tomorrow.
When I look back on today,
I have no sorrow.

Right or wrong, choices I will make,
Every day, for my own sake
Action over inaction
Purpose, pain and passion
Learning to unlearn and relearn
Prepared for what awaits me,
Around every corner I turn.

Support each other,
and grow together.
Build relations,
and bridge nations.

Live your legacy.
There's no fallacy.
Achieving success, happier than ever.
Reducing our stress in this joyful endeavor.
The future is now our present.
Nimbly unwrap your return on investment.
Divya Parekh

THE ENTREPRENEUR'S GARDEN

I had trouble sleeping the night after I met Dee. I felt like I did when I was a little girl trying to go to bed on Christmas Eve. I sprang out of bed as soon as my eyes opened. For the last couple of weeks, I hit the snooze alarm and didn't want to venture out. Today was different!

Although I looked forward to our first meeting, I was also feeling apprehensive about it. The butterflies were attacking my stomach in waves as I walked towards Dee's home. What am I doing? Fortunately, my fears vanished as soon as Dee flung open the door. She gave me a big smile, and I felt I was with an old friend. I made a mental note of the power of a friendly smile.

"Good morning, Sally," she said. "I am glad to see you don't mind the early hour. Why don't we walk along the beach? I do my best thinking there."

"That sounds good to me," I responded. "It's a beautiful morning."

We started walking side by side on the beach, feeling the gentle ocean breeze against our faces. The warmth of the sun struggled to make its way through the clouds. She asked me a few questions about my business, and I gave her a broad overview of what I did and my last several years. Dee then asked, "Did you get a chance to think about those questions I gave you last night?"

"I certainly did. The questions seemed so obvious, but they made me reflect deeply about my business."

"What did you come up with?"

I gave her a half-hearted smile. "That if I don't change what I am doing, I'm not going to succeed, or even be happy trying to grow my business."

"There you go, Sally. By asking yourself thought provoking questions and thinking through the answers, you are starting to grow your relationship with yourself."

"I remember you telling me that the key to being a successful entrepreneur is relationships."

"Yes, which is why we are starting with the relationship you must have with yourself." She began ticking off with her fingers. "Then we will be exploring your relationship with time, money, people, market, team, partners, death, legacy, and results. We will look at how you work with the excellent results of mastering these relationships. Trust me; by the time we finish you will be the success you want to be."

"Wow, that sounds very intense," I said, revealing the tiny bit of dread that seeped into my voice.

"Don't worry, dear. Rome was not built in a day, as they say. Building relationships is a process and will take time. Some of these relationships will take you longer to get a handle on than others. You will find that you are already strong in some of the relationships, and this process will give you the opportunity to strengthen them. Everybody is different."

"Okay, I can understand that. So what can you tell me about this relationship with myself that I have to start with?"

Dee considered the question for a moment and said, "First, we all have to figure out who we want to be. That means we have to take a hard look at our values, passions, and what we think our purpose is in life. Similar to the questions I asked you last night, these are things we kind of know about, but we rarely go through the process of thoroughly thinking them through. That is unless someone directly asks you about them." Dee gave another big smile. "That's my job."

I pondered on what she said. After a minute of walking on the sand, I responded, "I think I know what drives my life, but since I am going a hundred miles an hour every day, I am unable to focus on questions."

"Let's say you are taking up gardening for the first time. As a beginner, you have to learn how to take care of your flowerbeds so that they grow properly. In the beginning, it is a forced activity because you are not used to the work. Later, watering, weeding, and the rest of the care become a part of you. Likewise, I want you to get to the point that your values, passions, and purpose are so automatic that they are a part of you," said Dee. "Once you are there, you will have a mindfulness about yourself that will be the foundation from which you can build everything else on." She abruptly changed the subject. "Did you take any biology in school, dear?"

"Back in high school," I said. "I avoided the sciences in college."

"Our brains are an incredible piece of design," said Dee. "The amygdala section of our mind secretes chemical neurotransmitters and stress hormones like adrenalin and cortisol. When we experience fear, this is where our 'fight or flight' response originates. When that happens, our ability to see a situation clearly becomes hazy. By having an acute mindfulness of who you are and what you believe in, you will have a firm platform to hang onto when things start getting crazy."

"I feel that I am conditioning myself to deal with problems," I said.

"And getting yourself ready for life," Dee chimed in quickly. "Athletes practice for countless hours for their sport. Mentally and emotionally, you have to do the same thing with yourself. There is more to it, though. By acquiring mindfulness about yourself, you will see that this mindset extends inward and outward. Not only will you become aware of your strengths and weaknesses, but you will naturally become aware of what other successful people do. You will be more open to learning from the habits and practices of successful people whom you admire. As your understanding of yourself gains depth, you will integrate the lessons in alignment with your values. Like any good process, you have to complete the first step - establish the relationship with the self - before you move on to the next step."

The Power of Values as Life Compass

We walked on for almost five minutes as I rolled this concept around in my brain. "Hmmm," I finally said, "I do see what you are saying. What exactly is the relationship with self?"

"Great question," Dee said. "Let me share the definition and elements of relationship with self with you. I see you brought a notebook with you. Let's sit for a few minutes so that you can write them down correctly. They are important. You see, your relationship with self is to know and understand your purpose and values. You use them to be sincerely authentic in everything you do. Whenever you are knocked off course, values will help bring you back to that authentic place. Now, let me give you some specifics about these concepts."

I diligently wrote down everything she said. It was something I consistently went back to whenever I needed to revisit my relationship with myself. The main points were:

- The Purpose is the grit, the 'WHY' that galvanizes your passion and allows you to make a difference.
- Your values are the principles that define what is important to you in life and work.
- Your values are the compass that determines your priorities in life, guide the direction of your life through focused decisions, and define the framework of your behavior.
- Align your words and actions with your values. Then, your values act as the measure of your success in life.

I asked Dee, "What happens when you deepen the relationship with self?"

Dee answered, "You arrive at a point where you dissolve the barriers you set up between your personal and professional self. What you want to be is consistently authentic in your thoughts, feelings, and actions in all facets of your life. You have accomplished that when you show up as the genuine *you* everywhere."

"That shouldn't be too hard. Don't people do that automatically?"

"Hardly!" Dee responded emphatically. "People tend to wear masks for the different things they do in life. They have one for family, one for work, maybe one for an organization where they volunteer their time. A person wastes a lot of energy that way and may have trouble deciding who he or she really is. To do this, you have to be willing to bring together your vulnerability, humility, confidence, power, grace, brilliance, and the entire spectrum that is you. Furthermore, you then have to consciously work at showing the real you with everything you do. After a while, what you may have to force in the beginning becomes natural."

"I suppose when I get to that point, it will be an easier way of doing things than I have been doing lately."

"Yes, dear," said Dee in her assuring manner, "it helps you to integrate all of your knowledge and experience. You become consistently authentic in your thoughts, feelings, and actions during all phases of your life. You will discover it is easier to bring your vulnerability and grit into play in positive ways. As you strive to have this relationship with yourself, you will realize that your business will reflect that authentic self. It will come through in your performance, marketing, products, services, results, and success!"

"That would be quite a feat to pull off!" I exclaimed.

"Yes, it will, but you have it in you to do it," said Dee. "It will get easier as you continuously practice doing this. Ten years ago, I helped someone in a similar position that you are in with your business. For kicks, he ran marathons. After about a year of working with him, he came back and said that when he started to have that consistent feeling of his real self in everything he did, it was akin to a runner's high."

"I guess it paid off for him."

"It certainly did. When you take down the borders between your professional and personal life, you will find yourself with more courage and confidence dealing with anything. It might be securing that big client you want, or walking across a room to talk to that cute guy you saw come in."

It was my turn to smile. "A guy…what a concept."

Dee giggled. "Life is not all about work, Sally. The world would be a sad place, or at least your life would be. I want you to start thinking of your life as an organic whole, not dividing it up into different sections."

Co-relation of Self-Relationship and Business Success

As I reflected on the relationship with self, it led me to ask Dee, "Why is the self-relationship essential to business success?"

"When you recognize and understand your values, you can make decisions and action plans aligned with them. When you do this, you connect to your inner core that brings you pure joy and happiness. You will experience a harmony with your thoughts, beliefs, intentions, and actions. Life will be more play than work."

"Developing this relationship will put me on the right track for my business?" I asked.

"Yes, it is the most precious gift that you can give yourself. It will set you free to realize your potential. You will have the greatest chance of achieving your financial and life success. Having a trusting relationship with yourself acts as a compass during times when you discover you are not aligning your decisions and actions with your values. It will help you navigate those times when you need a clear direction in what you are doing."

I asked her, "When did you realize this was important to you?"

Dee composed her thoughts and told me, "I can't say I was in alignment with my values early in my career. It was causing me a great deal of grief. I realized that I needed to determine what my values were. When I did this, I was able to bring consistency to my work and clients. Then it occurred to me that I needed to be consistent in who I was with my values in every facet of my life. There wasn't a Dee for work, and a different Dee for family, and still another Dee for friends. There was just Dee."

"Can you give me an example of how this had a direct impact on your business?" I asked.

"In the early days of my career, money was a concern. Because of that, I would take on clients who quibbled about the pricing and did not understand the value I provided them. Not only did they not take measures that we had planned together to further their career or business, but they would also cancel their sessions more often than not. When we did meet, they would want to linger around after the session was over saying how much they needed a few additional minutes. Because I was not clear about my values, I agreed to coach them, and they became energy vampires. The misalignment between my clients and me directly affected my coaching, performance, and happiness. I always felt I was not giving enough. It all came down to not valuing myself properly. It had nothing to do with them. I was projecting the problems I had with myself on my clients."

Understanding the How Model

"How did you manage to figure all that out?" I asked.

"I had my mentor. With her guidance, I gained clarity on my vision, mission, and values. Let me give you my interpretation of those words. Vision is the long-term view, the mission is your plan, and values drive your decisions and actions as we talked earlier. I decided that I wanted to be part of a worthy cause and live by my values. I wanted to be my authentic self regardless if I was talking to a CEO, a colleague, or a custodian. By doing that consistently, I started trusting myself more and more. In turn, people believed me. Trust is the currency of relationships."

Dee fell silent for a few minutes. I looked at her and saw that she was deep in thought. Finally breaking the silence, I asked, "How did you change your approach?"

"First, I had to decide that I was going to be consistently authentic. I started working strategically with my coaches. I meditated and reflected on my past successes. I examined how I had accomplished seemingly impossible tasks several times earlier in my career. As I reflected, meditated, and researched, I discovered a pattern emerging. My coach told me, 'Dee, why don't you systematize it into a system? If it has helped you over the years to achieve your success, it can help so many other people. Why are you keeping your potential and true value from them?'"

"Is that why you are helping me on the beach this morning?"

"That's right. I took my coach's advice."

"In all of my wrestling with my business, I never considered that I first had to have a self-relationship," I said. "What do I need to do to achieve it?"

Starting to walk along the waterline again, Dee said, "First, you need to figure out where are you right now in connection with all nine relationships. Use the Enneagon Tool. You can easily find it on the Internet at Success. divyaparekh.com/assessment."

I asked Dee, "When can I take the assessment?"

Dee looked at my face eager with anticipation and said, "How about now?"

We sat down on the beach, and I pulled out my phone. I found the link and started to take the assessment. I saw that I was strong in several areas and needed to shorten the gap in few. I reflected on the assessment's results and talked with Dee about it.

She said, "This is where you have to seriously consider how to amplify your strengths and how to bridge the gap between 'where you are' and 'where you want to be.' For personal development, you meet yourself where you are at; in business, you meet your connections where they are at."

"So I need to have clarity where I am at, as well as whoever I am dealing with?"

"That's correct, Sally. If you want to bring your business up to a higher level, you have to bring yourself up to that place. Otherwise, frustration and being overwhelmed are your routine companions."

"I'm too familiar with those feelings," I said. "I want to learn how to get past that."

Dee looked at me and said, "You are one courageous woman. While we leverage your strengths, it is important to direct your efforts in the right direction to minimize frustration. You can learn from people you admire and weave the lessons into the fabric of your life. It will shorten the time towards your success because you are avoiding the traps that they have already avoided or ironed out. Sally, are you in entrepreneurship for the long term or the short term?"

"I want to be a total entrepreneur, Dee. I don't want to limit myself."

"Then you need to have a marathon mentality rather than a sprint mentality. An important factor to keep in mind is that when you run this marathon, you are running for yourself and for making an impact on others. The remarkable thing is that once you know your values, creating a vision for your business is relatively straightforward. We will talk about creating vision when we talk about your relationship with time."

"Before we get to that one, how do I determine my values correctly?"

"You identify your values by using the Values Exercise[1]. Align your actions with your values, and you will feel good about your decisions. Alignment of actions and values will boost your energy and confidence."

"Is this relationship with self an ongoing process?"

"Sally, you know life throws you lemons and gives you access to sugar to make lemonade. We have to keep working on this process. I'm 84 years old, and I still work at it every day."

"In your experience, are there any values I should lean on more than others? Or for that matter, any I should discount?"

"I have learned that if you have the value of love and service to others, you will love and serve everyone regardless of who it is. Remember that you cannot serve those who are not ready to be served. The principle of love and service proves invaluable over time. As for other values, that is what you have to examine in yourself."

As Dee continued to explain, I listened with rapt attention and took extensive notes. As she finished talking, she seemed a little exhausted. After taking a deep breath and closing her eyes for few minutes, she opened her eyes and said with a broad smile, "I can't wait to see the first chapter of this book. Even more importantly, I am looking forward to how strengthening your relationship with self helps you in your business. Now, why don't we head back to the house? I'm feeling a bit tired. You know, I'm not 80 anymore!"

I laughed, and we headed back to her home. When I left her at the door, Dee said, "Give this some time to form in your mind firmly. Start working on it. We'll get together for our next session when you are ready. Don't hesitate to call me with any questions."

Over the next couple of months, I worked on solidifying the relationship with myself. I did take Dee up on her invitation and asked her some questions as I was struggling with the process. Here I will summarize some key points that helped me crystallize my thinking.

---

[1]   Reference the exercise post summation at end of chapter.

Mindfulness

Mindfulness is a conscious effort to know yourself. As a definition, mindfulness is a conscious choice of living in the present, guided by value-based decisions and non-judgments. Mindfulness is also living with grace. As we focus on the dance of the present, grace weaves its way into day-to-day activities and relationships.

Mindfulness brings self-awareness without judgment. Knowing yourself is the foundation of authenticity. Non-judgment allows you to be accepting of your strengths and limitations. You are open to finding out about your blind spots and emotional hindrances. You can turn them into assets driven by values and support of friends and mentors. Mindfulness equips you with the desire of growth allowing you to learn from your life experiences - failures and successes alike - while retaining humility.

Mindfulness is a significant characteristic of a successful entrepreneur because it allows you to observe people without judgment. By observing without judgment, you become aware of the needs, values, and wants of others. It enables you to strategize and deliver under pressure while being thoughtful of everyone including yourself, your team, and your customers. You can put systems and processes in place to help you move forward. If you are not mindful of your strengths and shortcomings, you can neither leverage your strengths nor get things done in areas where you are deficient. For example, if marketing is not your suit, then you can accelerate your business by outsourcing it, collaborating, or bartering with someone.

Authenticity

Authenticity means being your real self in personality and character, despite external pressures. You do not find a need to don a mask. Because you take the "real you" everywhere, your authenticity is reflected in your speech and actions as well. When you are authentic, it will show through in all aspects of your interactions with others.

When people do business with others that they see are authentic in their dealings, they will trust them. As a result, business growth is inevitable.

Always observe your personal actions and thoughts as you interact with people that work with you, individuals who partner with you, or your customers. If you take shortcuts or do not respect others, people start losing their trust in you. Some on the team may follow your lead because they think it is okay to do what the boss does. They might check out mentally or emotionally as the well of inspiration dries out. As a result, nothing is getting done the right way, and business suffers.

Summation

The result of living with mindfulness is showing up authentically in every interaction. Because you show up as yourself, you brand yourself. Branding in today's world is important as your clients find you based on how you position yourself. The key is to show yourself consistently. Unswerving practice breeds mastery, which in turn increases passion! Your trust in yourself deepens. The trust your friends, team, partners, and clients have in you increases as well.

Strive for transparency and honesty in all aspects of business. Often we tend to look at the rearview mirror of the past, but forget the larger windshield of the present that allows us a grander view of our lives. It is important to let go of the rear view mirror to allow for growth. As we enter the relations field, it begins with the relationship with yourself. All of us experience the constancy of change. Here, we need the congruence of our values despite the external turbulences. When we move beyond our beliefs, thoughts, and state of being, we make value-based decisions. Value-based decisions align with the present and the future you want because they surpass perspectives and experiences.

Defining Your Values Exercise:

"Your beliefs become your thoughts. Your thoughts become your words. Your words become your actions. Your actions become your habits. Your habits become your values. Your values become your destiny" - Mahatma Gandhi

Grab a notebook. It's time to do some writing. Give yourself a quiet space with no distractions, and at least a weekend to determine your values.

Step 1 Think through and describe the following questions in both your personal and professional life in detail:

1. What were your three greatest achievements?

2. What were your achievements that other people were proud of?

3. Write three projects or activities or tasks you have completed efficiently.

4. Write three decisions that you have never regretted.

5. Write the three happiest moments of your life. Who was with you at the time?

6. Write the three most meaningful experiences of your life. Who was with you at the time?

7. What are any common themes that you can identify?

Step 2 Reflect why each experience was truly meaningful and memorable. What top ten tips would you give to your younger self so that your achievements and memorable moments would be more than what you remember?

Step 3 Reflect on Step 2 and confirm if those 10 tips are your top ten values.

Step 4 Now, you have the opportunity to test your values. Make a decision based on your values. How does the decision make you feel? If it feels right, you are on the right track. Your values might adjust and develop over time as you grow and as your life's circumstances change. For example, when you go from being a single 21-year old to beginning a family, you will most likely change your values.

Notes on the Enneagon Business Success Tool: You can access Enneagon Tool at **Success.divyaparekh.com/assessment**

1. The tool measures the gap between where you are and where you want to be in all the Relationship Essentials.

2. Gaps in any of the Relationship Essentials cause internal and external struggles impacting performance.

3. Entrepreneurs experience stress in proportion to the gap chasm (bigger the gap, the more stress).

4. Struggles influence mental and emotional resilience, thereby affecting performance and causing barriers to success.

5. The gap for any Relationship Essential can be reduced through steps shared in each chapter.

CHAPTER 3

TIME IS THE CURRENCY OF LIFE

Time lost is life lost, opportunity lost, value lost, and money lost. Invest in time wisely!
Divya Parekh

The next few months were eventful. I spent a great deal of time determining my relationship with self. It was an eye-opening experience. I did have a couple brief beach meetings with Dee to help me clarify my thinking and we exchanged a few emails and phone calls. I experienced a few shaky moments in figuring out my values[2] and how to incorporate them into my business practices. Dee reminded me that it was an ongoing process and that helped me settle down. I realized that since trust is one of my values, I preferred dealing with people I trust.

I discovered that as I worked consistently to operate my business in line with my values, good things started happening. I found myself becoming happier with the work I was doing and the clients I was helping. I felt more confident in many aspects of my daily routine. I liked having the anchor of my values in making business decisions as I increased my business success.

I related how I was feeling to Dee in an email, and she replied. "I think you are ready to take on the next relationship. Let's meet next week on Saturday morning. In the meantime, I want you to answer these questions for yourself:

---

[2]   Defining Your Value exercise from Chapter 2

1. Where do you expect your business to be in two, five, and ten years from now?

2. What will business look like if you continue to manage time as you do now?

3. Are you doing anything today for your business to be where it needs to be tomorrow?

4. With all the work you have as an entrepreneur, do you get all the work done efficiently and without stress?

5. How do you prioritize your tasks when unexpected developments occur during the day?"

Early on Saturday morning, I was at Dee's door. Unlike the first morning when I came here, I no longer had butterflies fluttering around inside. I had confidence in working with Dee right from the beginning, but after implementing her first lesson, I now saw how her ideas translated into practical applications. Furthermore, it worked!

She came out with her usual smile. "I can see, Sally, that your relationship with self has yielded some good results already. Your email updates have been very encouraging." She peered at me intently over her glasses. "You look more relaxed than you did when we first met."

I laughed at that. "I don't know about relaxed, but I don't seem to be struggling as much with every single thing in my business right now. I am more focused now as I continue to implement self-relationship tools."

"You are feeling comfortable with the choices you are making as you live by your values?" Dee inquired.

"Yes, I am," I said proudly. "In fact, I started the book I am writing about the lessons you are teaching me because it feeds my passion for helping others. Doing that is forcing me to think more intently than I have done in the past. The added concentration of constructing the book is turning out to be very helpful."

"I'm glad to hear that, Sally. Remember as we continue together, you will see that no one concept is ever independent of one another. You are teaching yourself that perception with your writing. Now then, did you have a chance to think about the questions I sent you?"

"I certainly did and found them to be very useful."

Dee smiled at that. "Sometimes we have to ask the right questions to come up with helpful answers."

I said, "I am beginning to understand that. Before we start with my answers, I wondered how many remarkable and memorable moments you have had over the years."

"You make me sound positively ancient, dear," Dee laughed. "It's like this, Sally. I have quite a few of those moments in my life. Sadly, I don't have enough because there are segments of my life that are totally blank. For me, the relationship with time is that I can say that I have lived my life the way I wanted at the end of every day. I will have memorable moments today as I do every day. I do not have any regrets. I wake up each morning, even at this age, ready to move forward with humility and grit."

I had to think about that for a few moments. I hoped once I reached Dee's age, I would have the same passion for life that she does. Then I slowly started to say, "I believe that when it comes to my business, I have always done pretty well with planning out my time. While I am sure I can improve on it, I have always been able to prioritize and map out my work. I know I want my business to create jobs for ten people in five years, and I want to have at least two companies at the ten year mark."

"That's great, Sally. Everybody has a different skill set. You know how to deal with some of the things I will talk to you about. I am helping enhance the knowledge you have and filling in the blanks where you need. I am sure you do well with time. However, I hear a 'but' in there."

I smiled at her and let out a big sigh. "The truth is that growing my business takes up most of my time leaving no time for myself."

Dee asked, "How productive is the time you put into your business?"

"I can't say that my time is very productive," I acknowledged. "I'm making money, but my business has reached a plateau. Even as I put more time into taking the business to the next level, I'm not going anywhere. I guess you can say that I am experiencing diminishing returns on the time I have been spending on growing my company. I am ready to learn how to be more efficient with my day. I want to carve out personal time before I burn myself out."

Time Relationship and Business

"Sally, I think it is important how we define time as it relates to being an entrepreneur. Your vision of where you want your company, or future companies, is time on a grand scale. Your daily schedule and routines are time on a short-term scale. The important thing to remember with either of them is that you have to be flexible first, and then adaptable with the changes that occur within each perspective. As much as we desire a simple life, nothing happens in a straight line. Things happen.

"Say you plant some vegetables. In the spring, it all seems simple. Till the earth, plant the seed, and watch everything grow. However, if you have an infestation of bugs, weeds, lack of rain, too much rain, you have to adjust your efforts for the extra work, in the hope of still having many fresh vegetables at harvest time. In business, how you manage your time is an important key to your productivity and profitability."

"I am fairly confident of my vision," I said. "Sometimes that daily schedule controls me rather than the other way around."

Dee chuckled. "Funny how that happens more often than it should. However, you *are* in control. Let's break it down this way. You need to know your vision, which you indicated you do. Remember that vision is what you want for your future. Furthermore, your values direct the journey. It defines the purpose of your business and what you want your business to achieve over time. The vision will be your primary guide and source of inspiration. Your mission, aligned with that vision, also communicates to all the purpose of your organization."

"Please explain more?" I asked.

Simply put, the mission informs others why your organization exists. When you write out a formal mission statement, it should answer the questions: what the business does, whom it serves, and how it fulfills your vision. As you answer the "how" you are articulating the systems and pieces that operate your business to achieve your vision. At this point, you organize both your personal and professional life. As an entrepreneur, they are going to be connected many times. If you do not organize one of them, one will bleed into the other. Developing the discipline to maintain focus so that you can bring any task to completion is also important. As you work on doing this, you will see that productivity and profit go hand-in-hand."

Why Time Relationship Is Important for Business

We sat down on a mound of sand. Looking out over the ocean, I tried to organize what Dee said in my mind. "I hear you talking that I have to be very conscious in my use of time as it relates to my business…and also my personal life?"

"That's right, Sally." She turned and looked intently at me. "Time is the most valuable currency of life. Once lost, it is gone forever. Lost time can translate into lost opportunities, missed connections, and lost destiny. Losing time means losing life because you have not lived the way you want to live. The key to understanding a relationship with time is knowing where you are in your life right now, and where you and your business is going to be in the long term."

"Is that why we first talked about relationship with self? Because I needed to know myself before I figure out where I want to be?"

"You got that right, Sally. In the relationship with self, we focused on your values. Now, your clear vision for your business future increases your confidence level and, therefore, the chances of achieving your goals increase tremendously. Because you know your vision and values, you will take actions that will bring you closer to your destination. You will find that you have fewer distractions and doubts as you concentrate on your goals."

I pulled out my notebook and listed the positive points Dee was relating to me, and what I believed the benefits would be for me. I wrote:

- Belief in yourself
- Clear sense of direction
- Open mind to possibilities
- More opportunities
- Greater ease and focus
- Renewed energy
- More productivity
- Self-commitment
- Success

Looking over my shoulder, Dee said, "You grasp the concept quite well. As an entrepreneur, I value my time. I plan my time for what to do, when to do it, and how to account for my activities in a way that generates income."

I asked, "Did it take you long to figure this out?"

"When I was starting out, Sally, people enjoyed coming to me to pick my brain on different matters. I was happy to do it because we helped each other out. However, helping is one thing and giving away your expertise is another. Plus, I struggled with time. I was so busy that every day I was booked solid. I was busy but rarely felt productive. Never think that being busy means productivity."

"How did you resolve the issue?" I inquired.

"I first had to realize that it was an issue…and a huge one. As an entrepreneur, I was overwhelmed and frustrated because I did everything myself from bookkeeping to coaching clients. I was the 'jack of all trades, master of none.' I realized that in life, we have risks to face, choices to make, and consequences to bear. I knew that a healthy relationship with time would result in business efficiency. I figured that keeping my joy and passion would lead to creativity and innovation in my company. If you mismanage your time, you are unable to create a stable identity for yourself because you didn't prioritize the important things in your life."

How to Strengthen Your Time Relationship

Dee continued. "When I decided to start coaching while in the corporate world, I had limited time to devote to my business and I was very meticulous in my approach. When I made the jump from corporate to entrepreneurship, I was euphoric about being on my dream journey. I thought I would have too much time on my hands. I quickly figured out that I didn't have the support systems in place you naturally have in a corporate job – the people, the technology, the systems, etc. I had to come up with a way to make sure I was as productive as possible."

"You were where I am now," I told her.

"Sally, I want to show you the prioritization matrix. It is a simple tool that challenges you to focus on what is important."

"How does it work?" I asked.

"You might want to write this down in your notebook," she said.

I did. Listening intently, I jotted down the prioritization matrix:

Make a list of your main activities to be completed.

Prioritize the activities as one of the following:

Urgent and Important Activities – These activities need prompt attention because they have an impact on your business. These may include appeasing an angry client, completing projects with deadlines, signing a contract for new clients.

Customer Value Added Activities or Primary Revenue Generating Activities – These activities result in payment from the client or revenue generation. Activities may include coaching clients, doing work for your clients, research for your clients, meditating before coaching session so that you can give your best to the client, etc. To know if an activity is customer value added, ask yourself, "If I do not do the task, will it impact my revenue or displease the client?"

Business Value Added Activity – Activity that will not generate income directly, but needs to be done for your business and will result in money eventually. Examples are personal development to improve performance, strategy and tactics development, project planning, results review, etc. The key is to take these activities and divide them into two categories – the activities I will do and the activities I will give to someone else. For example, you may be good at writing blogs, but you are not great at website maintenance. Then you decide to work on your blog and outsource, barter, or trade services for website development and maintenance.

Non-value Added Activity. This fourth type of activity covers anything that is not contributing to your business. For example, you spend time contributing to Facebook groups that are not generating any collaborations or revenue.

As I finished writing, Dee said, "It is important to remember that the right information translated into right actions at the right time yield right results and ultimately, the revenue you want. With a clear business vision, you know what activities you are an expert at and what activities you can delegate. Doing so will make categorizing and prioritizing your day much easier!"

I looked down at my notes. "We covered a lot of information."

Dee said, "You are right. Let's walk back to the house. I will share with you a time management program I created. As you begin applying time efficiency tools, you will see yourself become more productive."

We casually walked back up the beach to her house chatting about life in general. Once there, she reached inside the door and gave me a file. "I can see you were ready for me," I said.

"Of course," she said with a twinkle in her eye, "it saves time."

I laughed and went back to my place. I sat it aside until later in the evening when I felt clear-headed. The first several pages talked in more detail about time, vision, and mission. I have taken the liberty of sharing Dee's further wisdom here.

Time

How people feel and think about time is as vast and varied as the number of minds that have lived on earth. It is important to think about business development over a short period. As a business owner, you want to think how your business will evolve over time. You need to plan for that to become a reality. Long term planning relates to developing your vision, while short-term planning involves your mission.

Vision

Visioning is the process of creating a picture in your mind of what you want for your business in the future. Visioning uses both the mental and physical tools of your mind and body, such as the thoughts and actions to create and realize your goals.

Experts have widely acknowledged that there is power in defining, declaring, and then committing to realizing your dreams. Your vision is the articulation of your desired future.

A clear prophecy will help you set the desired course. Without this direction to guide us, we often fail to acquire the quality of life we want and expect.

By following the visioning exercise, you will be well on your way to determining and realizing your vision for your business!

Exercise

The goal is to identify your vision goals for the future. This exercise helps you to connect with what you want, as opposed to what you think you should do. When doing this exercise, balance what you would love to have happen for your business with what you believe can happen.

Instructions:
Complete the table to fit your needs. Note: Be honest with yourself. Write what reflects YOU, not what others think about you!

1. You can use the table and put in 1, 2, 5, 10, or 15 years from now. Pretend that it is X year from now, and you are forwarding your vision table to someone you care about and who would want to celebrate your success. Include the key elements of your business that you want to grow. The business elements are finances, sales, marketing, management, culture, team development, leadership, customer care, technology, product and content development, legal, etc.

2. Share what has transpired and what you have accomplished during the x year in your business.

Blank Table

Business Element	Present State	Future State (After X Year(s) from Today)
Significant Areas in Business/Career		

Example of Sally's Table

Business Element	Present State	Future State After 5 Years from Now
Significant Areas in Business/Career		
Revenue per year	One Hundred Thousand Dollars	One million Dollars

The key is not to feel that your answers have to be perfect. Too many people let themselves become paralyzed by thinking that they have to get it "right." There is no right. There is just you and your dreams, finally written down on paper.

After you have completed this process, you will have many revelations and ideas on the topics you were exploring. Some may be unexpected surprises. Do not let this overwhelm you. Just sit with it, and give yourself time to absorb and reflect upon your newfound discoveries.

Effective Planning – Mission

The Mission, in practical terms, is robust and goal oriented. The Mission is the What, Who, and How of the organization or business. For example, at Sally's Consulting Services, our mission is to be a world-class business consulting service provider. Our organizational culture nurtures our teams and partners to provide extraordinary consulting to women entrepreneurs.

Ok, so now you have a much clearer picture of what you want for your business, what matters most, and where you would like to be. Congratulations, you've done some excellent work! Now let's map out a path to follow or set goals so you may achieve your vision.

Remember that life is a marathon, not a drag race. Don't create additional pressures by pushing yourself to accomplish too much, too soon. Planning is supposed to be fun! This is about you pursuing the most important things in your life. So take it easy and pick a couple of areas that you want to go after first. Planning involves starting out with the end date in mind, what a project looks like, and breaking it down into smaller areas you can act on.

A project plan for each sub-area has objectives, strategy, tactics, and tasks laid out to achieve your goals in a particular time frame. Then you take the plan and work it backward to list your tasks to accomplish it by quarter, month, week, and finally, the daily duties. Allocate time for the tasks while prioritizing the tasks. Be sure to include measurement checkpoints and progress criteria to know that you are on track for project completion. Manifest those, and then come back to your list and pick a couple of more goals to achieve. By approaching it systematically, you will get where you want quickly and easily.

Efficient Execution

Knowing you values and vision helps you understand what you believe in and what is important to you. As a result, you will own your responsibility and know what you will do and what you will not do.

Summation – Impact to Business

When you work on your relationship with time, you will find yourself working more efficiently. Running and growing your business will become more fun as you find yourself less frustrated and stressed out. By following the concepts that Dee laid out in this chapter, you will discover that you are methodically planning your business. At the same time, you are thinking about how to best utilize your time in the short-term and for the future growth of your business. As you embark on this discipline, you will find that not only your revenue is rising, but you also have an increase in the quality of your lifestyle.

Action Exercise

1. Create a list of tasks on Sunday evening that you need to do for the upcoming week.

2. Label the activities and prioritize them.

3. Decide which activities you are going to do.

4. Schedule these activities on the calendar.

5. As you prepare your calendar, remember to schedule stressful activities with breaks.

6. Delegate, if you can.

7. Include hard start and stop times.

8. Ensure that you include time to recharge. Figure out what is most important for you to recharge - for example, spending time with your family, exercising, etc.

9. At the end of the day, evaluate your day regarding productivity.

10. Write down what worked well and what you can improve.

CHAPTER 4

THE MONEY CONUNDRUM

Money provides you the freedom to live the lifestyle you desire so that you can serve others. Do so with a humble spirit and make a positive impact.

Divya Parekh

A little over two months went by when I received this email from Dee:

I am thrilled to hear that you have made such great strides with your time relationship. It gives me joy to know that that you have become excellent with using your time wisely and even carving out some personal space for yourself. I was especially interested in your recount of attracting more potential clients who are in tune with your values. I believe that comes from optimizing your efforts of knowing yourself better and managing your time wisely while continuing to leverage your existing strengths.

However, I did laugh when you expressed surprise at how much more money you brought in last month compared to your previous months. It is a nice problem to have, and it shows me that it is time to meet up again. Having more money falls in line with the next relationship that we are ready to explore further: your relationship with money.

As usual, I want you to do some thinking on the subject before we get together:

1. Do you lower your service prices to overcome client objections?

2. What progress elements of financial success do you track?

3. What does money represent to you?

4. What do you plan to earn in one year?

5. *How do you track and manage your finances - for example, monthly operations cost, budget, expenses, etc.?*

6. *Do you know your business numbers?*

Inform me when you want to meet up, Sally. I am in Chicago now, but will be home by the weekend.

Waiting for the agent to finish the paperwork for my new high-end office, I smiled as I read Dee's email on my phone. It couldn't have been better timing to hear from her, as I thought of how proud she would be of me having this beautiful office. After meeting with a corporate client earlier in the week, I realized that my office space needed upgrading. I decided to invest some of my additional income into renting a place that would make a good impression.

Looking up, I saw that the agent was still preparing my papers. I quickly emailed Dee back telling her that I would be glad to see her on Sunday. That gave me four days to prepare for our conversation. The next several days flew by, and I felt that I was accomplishing critical and important business tasks with ease. I was certainly feeling less overwhelmed than previously. I had taken Dee's relationship with time advice to heart, and it started paying off almost right away. I was always fairly good at managing my time, but Dee helped me prioritize my business activities, and I started to see the results.

As usual, I looked forward to seeing her. Walking up to her door, I felt total anticipation instead of any trepidation. When she came outside, I hugged her and said, "It is so good to see you again!"

She hugged back and said, "That is a pleasant greeting after traveling about for the last two weeks." She took me by the shoulders and backed up an arm's length. "My, you have a beautiful twinkle in your eye, Sally. I assume you are enjoying how things have been turning out?"

I laughed. "It is gratifying to see progress in certain aspects of my business."

"Fill me in on what you have been doing," said Dee.

We walked along the beach as I gathered my thoughts. I learned that Dee appreciated succinct feedback as opposed to the rambling conversations I had with her at the beginning. "Well, as I told you in some of my emails, I brought on a few new clients in the past month or two. The new clients are certainly more in line with the type of people I want to work with and I know I can provide them my best service. By the same token, I have divested myself of a few clients. I believe I did it tactfully, but I didn't think we were a very good fit together. I seem to be getting to an excellent place concerning the work I am doing for others."

"What has that done for you?" asked Dee.

"As I mentioned, I am making more money than ever before," I replied with a big grin. "I also enjoy my work more. I don't know if I am 100% there yet, but I am getting my passion back for what I do!"

"That's fantastic!" said Dee enthusiastically. "I know when we first met you desperately wanted to get the passion back for your career. Now you are beginning to see as you practice the relationships I share with you that your values allow you to focus on your career and personal life. This is a good time to bring up your relationship with money," Dee said. "Sally, you keep going on this track, and it is only going to get better. I want to make sure you are comfortable with the money that will be flowing into your life."

"I never thought more money would be a problem," I said with a smile.

"Most people don't, dear. However, people can have a complicated relationship with money. Most people have heard that money is the root of all evil. That is not true. However, what we do with money, can be."

"I am not sure I understand what you mean. Can you explain that?" I asked.

"You are doing what I did at your age. I started changing some ways I was conducting business, and the results were, frankly, more than I dreamed of." It was Dee's turn to laugh. "And I had some pretty big dreams back then!"

"What happened?"

"I went down the same road that many young people do when they start making a decent income," Dee explained. "I reinvested the money in my business. First, I upgraded the technology I was using. Then, instead of looking for an economical and serviceable office, I rented a beautiful office with a great ambiance that was out of my budget. I shopped in some of the finer clothing stores as I upgraded my wardrobe to what I thought a successful entrepreneur should wear."

I inwardly shuddered at her mention of going for a high-end office.

"I made what I thought were investments in my business," she continued. "I did some cutting edge self-improvement plans, hired a marketing consultant, and took on a few employees to delegate the jobs that I did not like or was not good at. I jumped the gun with some of the things I did when my income went up. I didn't realize that there are up and down business cycles, contingencies, and emergencies that I needed to be prepared for. I tried to do too many things too soon, and life caught me unprepared. That's the lesson I want to pass on."

Suddenly, I stopped on the beach and looked at Dee. She looked at me intently and said, "You have done some of the same things, right?"

"Uh…well… I did just lease an office in a lovely building in an affluent business district. I have to admit that I have been seriously considering about all the costly mistakes that you shared with me. Also, I recently acquired an expensive automated customer relationship management system so that my business gets a jumpstart."

What Is the Relationship with Money?

She patted me on the arm as we walked. "It is crucial to think about what your relationship with money is, especially when you start having some additional funds come in. It's great to earn it, but it is better to understand early on how to discipline yourself in its use. What you do with money is the most important component of your relationship with it. I have found nothing illustrates more of a person's nature than what they do with money, particularly when they have either an extreme abundance or scarcity of it. I think you see by now that you need to connect your business self and personal life for you to have balance. This connection carries over to money. Your money mindset allows you to know what having money means and knowing that money is not evil. It allows you the freedom to be mindfully aware of the present moment while knowing that our decisions and actions determine the results."

"I see how I need to connect my values with money as well." I added.

"Exactly," said Dee. "These relationships do not stand alone. In some fashion, they all interrelate with one another. Your money mindset is going to determine the league you play in. If you think small, you are going to work with clients who want to play in a minor league. If you believe that the sky is the limit for your business growth, your efforts will focus on clients who want you to help them grow to the next level. When you bring all your personal values into your work, your business will grow exponentially.

"It's like deciding if you want to be a gardener or a farmer. Pretend you have bought a house with a large acreage land and are ready to cultivate it. You have to make a mindful decision of whether you just want a little vegetable patch on the side of your home, or go all out and work the land to produce food for other people."

"I have experienced that a little already, Dee. I have been evaluating how I want to structure my future in regards to how big I want to be."

"Good thinking," Dee told me. "I'm glad you are taking the initiative on that. However, that's only part of it. As a business owner, you have to become comfortable talking, learning, and managing your money. You have to develop a disciplined money mindset while you are executing your business plan. If you are able to do this with humility while maintaining a giving attitude to others, you will find yourself living with a freedom and a quality lifestyle that your money will bring you.

We walked deep in thought as I mulled over what Dee had said. After some time, I looked at her and said, "I think this is what I am hearing:

Being prudent about money means:

- Having money is okay.
- Working for money is okay with a humble mindset and a 'ready to serve' attitude.
- Having the quality lifestyle you want is okay.
- Having the freedom that money provides so that you become a giver and serve more people is okay.
- Having money to be a giver and make a difference in other people's lives is okay.
- Hoarding money for personal use only, or to use it as a source of power over others, is NOT okay."

As I was speaking, Dee was nodding her head vigorously. I felt a wave of pride rise within me.

Why the Relationship with Money Is Important

"It is important to examine your relationship with money, and to see why it matters in business," Dee instructed. "You will want to look at every financial condition, including debt, liabilities, assets, and owners' equity – and how it relates to your vision, mission, and goals.

"Will that examination process help me develop my mindset on money?" I asked.

"It is the first step," Dee said. "Accountants work with what they call the GAAP. That stands for 'Generally Accepted Accounting Principles.' Those standard accounting principles are important in properly running your business, as they are the commonly accepted ways of recording and reporting accounting information. It is basically a simple formula for figuring out your profit after deducting expenses from sales. The formula makes perfect sense. By the way, it is a good idea to secure a knowledgeable accountant early on. Let that person grow with you and your business."

"Yes, I am aware of that," I responded. "I took a couple of basic accounting courses in college. I figure I will look for someone to help with the actual accounting as my business grows."

"I am glad you realize that, Sally. Accounting is certainly necessary for running successful companies, but your relationship with money needs to go way beyond the spreadsheet. Money has a way of affecting our emotions. We act on our feelings and emotions and then make an effort to justify it logically. When we understand our attitude towards money, it prepares us to handle the emotions that will emerge during the ups and downs of business."

Dee thought for a moment and then continued. "For example, I have seen entrepreneurs who are too busy worrying about money to think about its ramifications. If you have a bad relationship with money, it will cost you and your company. If you have a cash flow that changes substantially from one month to another, you will find yourself doing things that you wouldn't normally do. When you have been in that position, do you offer discounts to clients to increase revenue? Then are you unhappy with yourself later?"

I looked down at the sand and sighed. "Yes and yes," I said.

"Are you ever hesitant to raise your prices because you are afraid of losing a client or do you get tired of chasing after prospects since they seem to cause more headaches than profits?"

"Guilty on both counts." I confessed.

Dee said, "Sally, you are not the only one. Most entrepreneurs do similar things. Your level of relationship with money reflects in your conversation with your prospects, clients, employees, and partners. Let me expand on this point with a story. When I settled on my mindset with money, I was good with the freedom it brought me, and it provided the lifestyle I wanted for my family and me. When I arrived at this point, I mindfully figured out the money challenges of my clients.

"One of my clients was eager to learn and grow, yet was not ready to work on her money mindset. Because I connected with her where she was at, we worked on self and money relationships together. Our working together enabled the client to be successful. The client was so thrilled with her success that she referred several people to me. If you are clear about money, you can mindfully figure out where your clients are in their handling of money and allow them to come to your level of thinking."

How Do You Achieve Your Relationship with Money

I asked Dee, "How did you help your client make the shift from having a weak relationship to a strong relationship with money?"

Dee said, "Whether it is for yourself or your client, the first question to ask is whether you are interested or invested in your business. Interested means you rent; invested means you own the house. One is casual, and the other is a commitment. Interested in your business involves the use of excuses to justify doing things you don't believe in. Invested means you have the attitude to do what it takes to achieve your goals. Sometimes we need to reprogram our brain to transition from being interested to being invested."

"I think I am invested in being an entrepreneur. Right?" I said.

"I think you are almost there," responded Dee. "Let me share another story with you. One of my clients was in the second year of business ownership. As she networked with other entrepreneurs, she became fascinated with the ideas, opportunities, and strategies that others were using. In her zeal and excitement, she wanted to try all of it. She invested money in many programs, thinking that they would help her. She had not yet developed her mindset and relationship with money, so she didn't always follow her values, mission, or vision. Also, she did not consider the time it would take to master all the programs. It didn't take long for her to run out of money, and the excitement turned to stress.

"This client had the skills and knowledge to make a positive impact in her career, but trying to do everything at once left her paralyzed, frustrated, and procrastinating on things she needed to do to keep her business going. She began to waver in her decisions on whether to be a private coach, join a company, take on a partner, continue on her own, focus on webinars, make videos, write books, hire people to build a team, or outsource. There were too many options. I worked with her to develop a concrete foundation about herself, time, and money. It took some work, but together we got her to the point of concentrating on building a strong financial groundwork for a solid business that provided her financial freedom. It all came together for her when she became comfortable with her relationship to money. It became her cornerstone. She now has about a dozen businesses under the umbrella of her main company."

I glanced up surprised to find ourselves back at Dee's home. I was so into our conversation that I didn't even remember turning around. I said, "We work to make money at our business, but now I understand how it goes much deeper. The values that we build our business on apply to everything. Money is one of those items you have to bring into the equation," I said.

Dee snorted. "Maybe. I'll leave that to the math majors. I would rather deal with people." She went over to a manila envelope she had secured under a flowerpot on her steps. "I wrote a few things down I've learned over the years. It is going to take you some time to digest this concept and figure out your relationship with money. Ease into it. I think this material will help with what we talked about." As she handed it to me, she continued with a twinkle in her eye. "Feel free to use it in your book," she finished with a smile.

"Thank you, as always. Am I ever going to leave here without a lot to think about?" I asked.

"Not if I am any good at this," she said with a smile. We embraced. "Now go home and get a handle on this. It is that important. I am going to take a nap. It takes me longer to recover when I go traveling these days. I have to rest up for a concert I'm going to later."

"A concert? Like classical music or something?"

"No, the Rolling Stones are in town. They are almost as old as me, but they still put on a great show. I look forward to the magnificent things that are going to happen to you, Sally, as you apply this one."

She gave a little wave and went inside. I headed to my car shaking my head. Not only were my thoughts filled with this new relationship I needed to take a serious look at, but it was hard to envision Dee in a Rolling Stone concert t-shirt at the show tonight.

I gave a great deal of thought to the day's session with Dee, what we talked about, and the material she gave me. As I took notes and boiled it down for my consumption, I came up with this to share with my readers.

1. Creating the Money Mindset

It is not about dreaming dreams; it is about achieving goals. Your emotions play a strong role in your success. Ultimately, it is up to you to decide whether you are interested or invested in yourself. The key is to challenge yourself. Find an accountability partner to hold you answerable so that you continue to expect the best from yourself. Strive for continuous learning, growth, and improvement rather than perfection. An accountability partner will help you monitor yourself as you continually explore these points:

1. Find the truth about how you feel about money – is it the root of all evil or is it a means to help others?

2. Discover if you believe that you are worthy of money and the freedom and independence it brings.

3. Learn what you think about your ability to make money.

4. Figure out the worth you place on the value you provide to people through your services or products.

5. See the value other people offer to you.

6. Keep the cyclical money flow circulating by seeing the value other people offer.

7. Invest in other people's services.

8. Converse with clients, partners, and your team about earning increases.

9. Develop your business plan and execute the plan. The business plan includes clarity about why you are creating it and making sure there is a secure connection between vision, values, goals, and business solutions to ensure intrinsic motivation for efficient execution.

2. Business Plan Elements:

Creating a business plan requires time. However, the key aspects to keep in mind are:

Business Description
At a minimum, include your products and/or services, the history of your field, current trends, your company's goals and objectives, and why your business is a success.

Products and Services
Highlight in detail your services or products for clients, the relevancy of your offerings to the market, and what it is that makes you stand out in the crowd.

Sales and Marketing
Sales and marketing involve knowing your ideal client and creating branding that connects with those clients. Provide samples of what you offer to your client before they make an investment in you. Know your ideal client (the next chapter will cover Relationship with Market). Explain how you will help your clients succeed.

Business Operations
Business operations determine how your business can function smoothly without you being deeply involved. It is about developing relationships with your staff, team(s) (Relationship with team, Chapter 7) or business partners (Relationship with partners, Chapter 8).

It is important to pay attention to your business location, whether it is brick and mortar or a virtual website. You may want to list the equipment that you need to run daily operations. It is about establishing systems and processes that support your business, team, and clients. It also involves describing your suppliers.

Discuss your finances and have money in the budget for routine and unexpected expenses. Since you might not have expertise in all areas of business, it is important to work with advisors, coaches, or consultants who help you manage your business, contributing to your overall business success. As your company grows, it may involve people in various positions in the hierarchy of responsibility that makes your company a phenomenal success. Also, keep in mind the future vision of your business so that you can invest accordingly and wisely.

Process for Creating a Money Management Discipline

1. Review your vision from Chapter 1. Using vision as a guide, map out the business growth you desire for the future. Construct a plan that you can stick to and one that motivates you.

2. The handling of money is necessary. When you know your numbers, including your monthly cash flow, net worth, liability, assets, budgets, payroll, outstanding loans, etc., you can keep your finger on the pulse of your business growth.

3. Business is investing money in revenue as well as focusing on profits so that you can pay your team and yourself. It is about ensuring that operational costs are manageable.

4. Review your expenses. Simplify and eliminate redundant expenses.

5. Getting your finances in order involves creating a dream team of a chartered accountant, bookkeeper (personal or automated software

like QuickBooks, FreshBooks, Quicken, etc.), financial planner, and an insurance broker. An investment planner supports entrepreneurs to help enterprises meet their long-term financial objectives. An insurance broker helps people find the right insurance policies to cover life and all business insurances.

Balance business growth, profit, and personal life at all times. Think of business as an end-to-end process where you are making profit while you grow.

Business Summation

All business owners and entrepreneurs want to make money. That is the goal of business. However, the concept of money and your relationship with it is paramount to understand. Why you are making money is as important as how you go about it.

First of all, you need to clearly see the value of what you are doing in your business or if you own more than one. When you have a firm understanding of this, you will increase your confidence in delivering value.

Figure out your relationship with money. Knowing this relationship will increase the trust you have in yourself to go after your dreams. It also allows you to become consistent in your personal and business decision. Clients and customers will know who you are through this consistency, and it will bring like-minded people to your door. When you firmly ingrain your relationship with money in your mind, emotions, and actions, your business will thrive.

Action Exercise:

1. Hire a CPA and bookkeeper or bookkeeping systems that are right for you.

2. A majority of entrepreneurs make spending decisions based on the money they have in the bank account. Plan to set up different bank accounts.

3. Strategically distribute the money in different accounts.

4. Establish the bank accounts as follows[3]:

   a. Account for income (much of which will be transferred to fund other accounts)

   b. Account for salary (payroll)

   c. Account for taxes

   d. Account for operating expenses

   e. Account for profits – put in the money for your first three months. Then you can take it from there.

   f. Account for unpredicted expenses for rainy day – emergency fund.

   g. Reinvestment

   h. Sharing with the community or charities.

---

[3] The different types of accounts were inspired by Profits First by Mike Michalowicz

CHAPTER 5

INTERLUDE

I have to say that for the first time since I met Dee, I wasn't skipping to her home in anticipation. In fact, it was more as if I had the weight of the world on my shoulders. The weather wasn't helping. Today, it was gloomy and lightly raining. It matched my mood completely.

As I raised my fist to knock on her door, Dee opened it wide. She had her usual sunny smile on her face and two steaming mugs in her hands. "Good morning, dear," she said. "Since it is raining, let's sit out on the porch and drink some tea."

I reached out and gratefully took one of the mugs. After following Dee through several rooms, we arrived at the large porch with comfortable furniture scattered around. The roof extended out over the area, so we were well protected. I saw we had a beautiful view of the ocean. As Dee indicated a chair for me to sit in across from her, she peered at me closely. "You seem to be upset today, Sally. What's wrong?"

I forced myself to smile. "It was just one of those weeks. Since we last got together a month ago, I have been doing fantastic with my relationship with time and money. I have made some changes in how I work based on everything we talked about, and it is paying off handsomely. I have even started bringing some people on board. Now I find that I have to manage people, and it's…it's…"

"Difficult," broke in Dee.

"I was going to say it is sucking the life out of me, but we'll go with difficult."

Dee gave a little chuckle. "One of the problems when you grow your company is that you deal with more people. When you start out, all you have to worry about is your clients. Then you have people you hire as employees or contract workers or consultants. Next you will be putting together teams. When you start other businesses, then you are multiplying all of those factors. It's like planting flowers at your house one spring, and they are so beautiful, you expand the following year. You keep doing this and after a few years, it looks like you turned your place into a nursery. All those flowers mean approaching your gardening duties differently than when you first started."

I took a healthy gulp of the tea. It was as if Dee was reading my mind. She certainly summed up my issues. With all those people in my future, I wondered if I was up to the task. Expressing my concerns to Dee, I said, "It's not only that. I am not sure if networking with people will help my business grow. I certainly don't want to fritter away my time. I don't have any to waste. Did you go through this?"

"Sally, all entrepreneurs go through it. It is inevitable as you grow your business and your brand. Did I panic when I realized it was happening to me? You better believe it."

"How did you figure your way through it?" I asked.

"Some of it was through trial and error. I had a few mentors I leaned on." Dee's face suddenly lit up. "I just thought of something that would be a big help to you. I'll be right back."

For someone over 80, she was spry and returned before I took another drink of tea. She had a large binder in her hands. She gave it to me and said, "This is a good lead into our next set of relationships - those that have to do with people. At one point when I was continually expanding my business, I put some materials together to share with my staff. Since our connections with people are the crux of any success we have in the entrepreneur world, I wanted my managers and employees to have a good background on the subject."

I leafed through it and looked at some of the subjects in the binder. "This is very much what I've been thinking about lately. Are you saying you had planned for us to start talking about this?"

"Yes. I was going to go into the separate relationships, but now that I think about it, it will probably be a good idea if you read this first. That way you will have a good foundation as we go deeper into the next group of relationships."

I held up the heavy binder. "It must have taken you some time to put this together."

"I was constantly refining it as technology and business changed. I always meant to put it out there as a book." She shrugged. "I never quite got around to it with everything else I was doing."

"Maybe I can incorporate it into my book," I said.

"That might work," Dee said. "I wanted to help others with it. If you think that would fit into your book, Sally, you have my blessing."

"Thank you, Dee. I look forward to diving into it."

"Let me make us some more tea, and then you can tell me about your last couple weeks," Dee said.

When I returned home, I felt the warmth of the talk spreading through me. The rain had picked up during the day, and it was pouring. I changed into sweats and curled up on the couch with Dee's material. Before I knew it, evening settled in, and I leaned back and closed the book. It was very useful information, and I knew how much help it would be. I wondered how it was going to lead to the next set of relationships Dee, and I were going to explore.

Because of its value, I do include it here. It will certainly help you as we discuss the relationships with people. Enjoy!

Networking – A "How To" Guide

Networking, as essential as it is to long-term success, can be quite confusing. However, once you learn effective ways to network, you can develop lasting personal and professional relationships that will benefit you in the long-term. Through the techniques listed here, you'll learn how to network in-house and outside of your company for maximum opportunities and exposure.

The Benefits of Networking

The term "networking" is thrown around frequently in the business world, and for good reason: learning how to create connections within your sphere of influence and outside of it is integral for positioning yourself for success. While not everyone is comfortable networking, by taking the time and energy to meet others both personally and professionally, you might even find networking enjoyable!

Entrepreneurs misunderstand networking to be socializing at networking events, focusing on collecting business cards, and making contacts with the intention of seeking potential clients. They sometimes feel that they spend too much time, energy, and effort in networking because somehow contacts do not pan out.

Failure is the most likely outcome because we as humans need to trust others before we become their clients or form a partnership. While there certainly can be a social aspect to networking - and obtaining contact information is vital - networking effectively involves a bit more.

In the long run, the power of networking is the distinction between a contact, connection, relationship, trusted collaborator, and community.

Let's look at basic definitions:

- Networking: It is the process of cultivating lasting business connections and developing relationships. Regular contact and follow-up are needed along with healthy give-and-take interaction. Networking is about making contacts, creating connections, building relationships, and establishing a circle of trusted collaborators who have your back. Essentially, it is about building a community that gives to each other and society. There are several definitions of networking. For our purposes, networking is the act of:

  a. having values and purpose;

  b. developing a plan to achieve the goal of building your community;

  c. having a mindset of giving and taking the action to create a supportive and interdependent system of independent individuals who are willing to exchange information, share resources, and build mutually beneficial relationships.

- Contact is a person or someone you know, but have not ventured into the realm of creating connections. It is important to know that not all contacts become connections. The connection is the result of making an effort and taking timely actions in a given period. It is important to know that not all connections lead to relationships.

- Relationships are about giving, building trust, and creating the experience through repeated actions (connections) over a prolonged period. For example, wishing someone a happy birthday, sharing a referral, or helping him or her with their event. One can say that some connections mature into relationships, but not all connections lead to relationships.
- Trusted collaborator is a relationship who has your back, your confidence, and your welfare at heart. One can say that some relationships mature into trusted collaborators, but not all relationships grow into a reliable collaborator.
- Collaboration progresses into a lifelong friendship where friends become family and part of your community where giving, loving, and growing together are a given.

Create a Solid Network

When looking for potential people to network with, it's necessary to consider who the right people are, where you can meet them, and how mutually you can support each other to reach their vision. It's also important to realize that networking involves making connections and building relationships, not just meeting people.

Where to find possible connections:

- Referrals: Ask people who are close to you to recommend others with whom you might share ideas. Those who know you best will likely want to encourage your success!
- Join groups: Volunteer opportunities, professional organizations, and hobby or religious groups can all be places to network. Sometimes you find people in your field even when you're looking outside of it!
- Attend events: Organized networking events may sound dull, but they're an excellent way to make connections with like-minded individuals. Attending community events that are in alignment with your vision is another way to meet people. Remember not to get

discouraged; while you might not make a connection at every event, you make zero connections sitting at home.

- Your circle of influence: Your circle of influence includes your contacts, business team that works with you or people you might outsource work to, and social media networks (Linked in, Facebook, Instagram, etc.). It might give the impression of time wasted, but making genuine connections with the right people in your circle of influence can lead to gaining information, great recommendations, and even new business opportunities.

Meet Strategic Alliance Partners

When two entrepreneurs or companies work together to accomplish a goal, they become alliance partners. However, whenever individuals choose to combine their gifts, tension can arise. This is why it's necessary to screen any persons or businesses you plan on working together.

Networking can prove highly useful to discern strategic alliances. When creating a strategic partnership, it's important for the relationship to benefit all parties involved. Also, it may be helpful to work with someone you already know. However, if you plan to collaborate with a new company or person, it's necessary to get to know them before putting your reputation and business on the line. Because so much is at stake, you must ask yourself what traits you require in a potential partner. One thing you can do is make a list of possible candidates to partner with who meet your list of required qualities. You can then reach out to the people and companies on your list as the need arises.

Generate Leads

When finding new business contacts and leads, networking is essential. Referrals from friends and family, social networking sites, and networking and community events are important. While networking may take time and effort, generating leads is imperative to a successful business and career.

When meeting with new business contacts and leads, it's important to display the value that you offer and inform them of your goals and/or product or service. It's also necessary to follow-up with leads. Let them know you value contact with them. Take the time to connect and you'll not only build a relationship with the individual, but you'll also create opportunities for mutual support.

Position Yourself

Positioning yourself as a reliable contact and a subject matter expert in your field is an essential part of networking. Once people know your expertise, they will begin to seek you out. As greater numbers of contacts work with you, your reputation and networking capabilities only continue to grow. You further your network's knowledge of your skills by self-promotion and publications. For example, by authoring articles on your area(s) of expertise, you attract readers, make new contacts, and establish yourself as an expert in your field.

Shared Knowledge

Networking in your circle of influence and expanding to new associations not only increases your visibility but also can lead to shared knowledge. By making connections, especially with those who have vast experience, you can learn about potential areas for error and ways to avoid those mistakes. Also, bouncing ideas off of fresh faces can lead you to have new ideas or look at old ones from a different perspective.

Improve Image

Networking allows you a significant modicum of control over your professional image. Sharing your knowledge and highlighting your successes shows your contacts that you know your area of expertise and are a valuable contact to have. Combined with ethical professional behavior, you'll be an asset to others. As you support them to succeed, they will in turn be happy to help you.

Why Networking

There are many reasons and benefits of networking. Meeting people and creating connections not only impacts your social groups and hobbies, but also can bring in great employees, partnerships, or assist in contributing to a support system. Networking teaches trust, improves your professional visibility, and gives you an edge in your field. When trying to bolster one's presence personally or professionally, networking is essential.

Learning to Trust

Trust is the key element to creating and maintaining contacts. Effective networking can be a fantastic way to learn how to build trust. When creating new connections, you're more likely to form business partnerships if you trust one another. Building trust to further relationships can be simple if you just follow a few simple steps:

- Be honest: If you're truthful, sincere, and straightforward, you'll gain respect and people will want to do business with you.
- Be consistent: Follow through with your actions and promises and act with integrity.
- Be helpful: Do your very best to meet the needs of your contacts and associates. By being helpful, you'll bolster your reputation and increase your success.

Increasing Visibility

Standing out is essential in today's competitive business market. Since there may be a multitude of qualified entrepreneurs for any given field, heightening your visibility is key to improving your professional success. There are many ways to stand out to potential clients and business partners:

- Give with the intention of adding value and making a positive impact.
- Update your professional profiles every so often to reflect any new changes.

- ○ Create content for professional publications.
- ○ Speak at public or in-house events.
- ○ Share your expertise via social media or a blog.
- ○ Ask questions of those who know more than you.
- ○ Promote news or happenings via social media, a blog, or word of mouth.
- ○ Volunteer for a related group or professional organization.

Gaining Advantages

Networking can provide you with insider benefits and information. When you have a network, you have people who know about people who may need your services or opportunities that may not be publicized or well-known. You also have a source of references within your network and can recommend one another for various projects.

Best Impressions

When meeting with potential clients or entrepreneurs, especially connections referred through your network, it's important to make a spectacular impression. After all, you're not only representing yourself; you're representing the individual who recommended you. To ensure that the meeting with the decision maker stands out:

- ○ Be groomed and wear professional or appropriate attire for the meeting.
- ○ Be polite and take note of your body language.
- ○ Be engaging and helpful.

Networking Obstacles

Many people face a variety of obstacles when networking, as in any other undertaking. However, it's important not to let these obstacles get you down. By learning how to handle them correctly or avoid them, you can excel at making connections and strengthening your business.

Personality Differences

We each have our personalities and some individual personalities mesh better than others do. Understanding potential personality conflicts and knowing how to handle them can help thwart this obstacle from affecting your networking.

Personality examples:

- Extroverted and social: These types often have many ideas and may need help focusing. They also appreciate validation, especially in front of others.
- Type A leaders: These people tend to be assertive. They tend to hold their company to a high standard and often want others to agree with them.
- Detailed planners: This group works better independently and may have difficulty seeing the "big picture" if they don't have all the details.
- Quiet introverts: These people often do better in one-on-one settings with few distractions, so it's often best to meet with them privately.

These are just a few of the personalities you may encounter. Additional research may help you to navigate various personalities even better[4].

Cultural Differences

As business continues to grow globally and workplaces become more diverse, you will likely encounter cultural differences when networking. To communicate efficiently and connect with people from various backgrounds, it's necessary that you understand potential obstacles and be sensitive to cultural standards and customs. Examples of potential barriers might be:

---

[4] Because we are committed to your success and want to give you a jumpstart, reach out to contact@divyaparkh.com for a complimentary personality assessment.

○ Language/Accent: When someone is speaking your native language, but may have an accent, listen carefully and use context clues. Also, if the individual speaks a language you haven't learned, a translator can be useful. Finally, learning new languages is always encouraged, especially if you're going to be doing business with someone or a company whose native language is different from your own.

○ Stereotypes: Be aware of any prejudices or stereotypes you have regarding other cultures or people. Make sure that you're not treating someone differently because of misconceptions.

○ Cultural Norms: Be aware that just because something is the norm or acceptable in your culture, does not mean that it's acceptable in other cultures. Research and learn about other cultures' standards and customs. For example, in some cultures, eye contact is discouraged or hugging may be inappropriate.

Personal Pride

One's pride can sometimes also be a barrier to effective networking. While it's usually a positive trait related to confidence, pride can also prevent people from asking for help from their network. Since the purpose of having a network is to make connections for mutual support and benefit, not asking for help undermines the point of developing a network.

Time Constraints

Networking requires diligent efforts of energy and time. Networking can easily be an afterthought when you get caught up in the tasks of day-to-day life. To avoid allowing networking to fall by the wayside, it is imperative that you schedule time on your calendar for networking and stick to it. Use this time to follow up with contacts, meet new people, update your professional social networking sites, send e-mails, or make phone calls. Networking doesn't have to be a massive time investment, and frankly it's more likely you'll stick with it if the timeframe is reasonable. Just 30 minutes a day can make a huge impact on the success of your relationships and networks.

Saying the Wrong Thing

People often misspeak when meeting new contacts, and this is one of the most disastrous actions that can impact a budding network. To avoid this obstacle, it's necessary to be prepared and to speak carefully. Practice new conversations by running them through your head or even speaking aloud. Observe your body language in a full-length mirror. Make a list of usable phrases and appropriate topics to reference. Finally, use impeccable manners when meeting new people and making connections. Additional tips include avoiding alcohol or other substances that may lead to looser behavior, avoid criticizing, and treat everyone with respect and courtesy.

While this may not help you avoid all miscommunications, these tips can certainly contribute to reducing them. Just remember that if you say the wrong thing to someone, always apologize immediately.

Networking in the Wrong Places

People often limit themselves unintentionally while networking because they become confused about how and where to make connections. While networking via social media is important, it's integral also to network in person. Choosing places to network that enhance and reflect your business and networking goals is also important. For example, networking at events put on by professional associations related to your field is far better than trying to make connections at vague meet-and-greets. Remember, it's not just about making contacts, it's about developing useful connections. This principle also applies to social networking. Joining professional Facebook groups or exploring people in your field using LinkedIn, for example, are practical ways to make new connections.

Fear of Rejection

While rejection is an unfortunate aspect of life, and occasionally of networking, not allowing fear of rejection to become an obstacle is important. While no one likes rejection, fear can keep people from trying to network, since avoidance is one response to fear. Be aware if you find yourself making excuses not to network, as this could be a sign of avoidance due to fear.

Networking Principles

In order to create a robust network of reliable connections, it's important to focus on four key areas: developing new contacts, organizing contacts, following up, and relationship building. Following these steps will ensure that you cultivate a strong professional network that will enable you to reach goals while helping others achieve theirs.

Develop Contacts

Meeting people may sound easy, but developing contacts can be hard work! However, don't let that discourage you. When making contact with someone, whether in person or online, find out his or her needs. Once you know this, you can share ways in which you can help.

When you meet

At the first contact, meet a person mindfully as it will enhance your intuitive experience about the individual. Usually, the gut reaction is often right. If the intuition is not favorable, keep an open mind because it is possible that the person may be having a bad day and may not be responsive due to reasons that have nothing to do with you or their personality.

The next step is to compartmentalize that it is about them, not you. Treat them with the RWD principle. Have an RWD Mindset:

- ○ Respect - Treat everyone with respect in the manner that you respect the person you admire the most.
- ○ Warmth - Show them the warmth and kindness you would show a friend.
- ○ Dignity - Give them the dignity they deserve as someone you will learn from as you interact and contribute to each other's lives.

Use active listening where you have emptied your mind out and are ready to know about them as they share themselves with you. If you discover synergy, then plan to have a conversation or meet them again.

Tips to Make Contacts:

- ○ Ask the potential contact about him/herself.
- ○ Actively listen.
- ○ Share how you can support them.
- ○ Discover commonalities, such as shared interests.

Once you have learned about the person and figured out how you can support them to grow personally or professionally, it will be easy to find out if they will:

- Be your friend.
- Be your joint venture partner who understands your ideal clients.
- Be your collaborator in a partnership to serve the same clients while complementing each other organically.
- Be part of your team as an internal team member or as an outsource possibility for specific services.
- Be your potential client. Once you become more familiar with their needs, you will be able to determine if they are your ideal client and you are the right person to serve them.
- Be in none of the categories and you wish them the best.

Formal Networking

Formal networking often revolves around an arranged or coordinated event, such as a luncheon, social event, meet and greet, or a networking event. The exact format and setup may vary with each organization. When planning to attend a formal networking event, it's often necessary to do a bit of homework, either on contacts you're likely to encounter or on the company itself. You need to have insight and talking points ready. Also, look professional and fresh, so take time in your appearance and presentation.

Informal Networking

Informal networking is much more widespread and frequently occurs in daily life. Connection with your team, partners, or a potential client by sending a couple of texts to a contact can be considered networking, as can having an impromptu lunch with an associate. The main difference between informal and formal networking opportunities is the degree of initiative. With formal events, you take the initiative to go and actively seek our potential contacts. With informal networking, however, the initiative is taken when you ask someone to join you. One of the benefits of informal networking over formal networking is that it's low-stakes and low-pressure. If someone declines your offer, you can always try again later or reach out to someone else.

Everyday Opportunities

It's also possible to network during your daily routine. In addition to asking someone to join you for lunch, you can also take leadership roles in organizations that you are a member of or where you volunteer. Some organizations may have mentoring opportunities or focus groups where you can participate. You can also increase networking opportunities on your own. Being the go-to person for professional information can bring the contacts to you.

Always Be Ready to Network

Since networking opportunities can occur anywhere at any time, it's necessary to be prepared. To stay prepared, it's important to:

- Have your elevator pitch or your three magic words when somebody asks you what you do.
- Continually pay attention to the people around you.
- Look and present as the professional that you are.
- Reach out to others through personal gestures.
- Stay on top of changes in your field.

Organize Your Contacts

Once you've made contacts, you'll want to keep their information at your fingertips, as this makes networking much easier.

Tips for Organization:

○ Choose a single, centralized location: Choose an easy to access location in which to list your contacts and their information. The location can be a physical space, such as an address book, or a digital space, such as a spreadsheet or e-mail contact list.

○ Make categories: To ensure that you don't get your professional contacts mixed up with your personal ones, creating categories for your contacts can be a great way to stay organized.

○ Take notes: In addition to creating categories, it can be very helpful to make notes for your contacts, such as where you met, the last time you reached out to them, their interests, or things that you can help them with.

Follow-Up

Meeting people and swapping contact information is useless without following up. This provides your contacts with individual attention and lets them know that you value their connection. It's best to follow-up shortly after meeting someone for the first time; e-mail, text, or phone call within 24 hours is appropriate. After the initial monitoring, connecting once or twice a month is acceptable. Do not rely on mass communication when following up, as it appears insincere.

Also, be aware that not everyone you connect with will desire to build a relationship. If after many attempts at contact on your end there has been no response, spend your time and energy elsewhere.

Relationship Building

Through communication, time, heart and mind share, you will likely build relationships with your connections. To avoid losing your contacts, it's important to maintain these relationships. To keep your professional relationships alive:

○ Reach out regularly: Whether it's a text, phone call, e-mail, or a quick lunch, reaching out at least once a month after initial contact helps keeps you connected to the contact.
○ Give individual attention: Everyone likes to feel important and valued. By giving one-on-one attention, even in an e-mail, it shows that you care about forming a relationship with that person. When you share your heart (caring) and mind (knowledge) with others to provide value, it makes a positive impact.
○ Limit your network: Since you cannot give hundreds of people individualized attention, limit your network to mutually beneficial contacts.

How to Build Networks

Networking can be done in a variety of mediums. Physical networking involves meeting people face-to-face, often by attending events. Social networking is done online using several different sites created specifically for this purpose. Finally, after meeting or obtaining new contacts, you can create a network referral list.

Physical Networking

Meeting people in person is how physical networking works. Physical networking is a highly effective way to network because, although it takes more effort than other methods, we are much more likely to remember someone we meet in person. It gives you the chance to engage face-to-face and make a strong first impression. You can meet people in person in many of the following scenarios:

○ Local volunteer opportunities
○ Professional organizations
○ Chapters of local businesses

- ○ Social groups or hobby groups
- ○ Networking events
- ○ Invite an unfamiliar co-worker to lunch

Interacting at Events

Great, you made it to the event. You are ready to meet people. Perhaps you conquered your fear of rejection and finally made it here. Before you begin to socialize, however, there are a few things you should know:

First, you need to talk to people you don't already know. While it can be comfortable to mingle with established contacts only, this doesn't create any new connections.

Second, notice how conversations are going. Does the person seem disinterested? Is the conversation not useful? While you don't want to behave rudely, it's okay to excuse yourself from a conversation that isn't going anywhere.

Social Networking Sites

Regardless of how you feel about Internet connections and online communication, it's standard in today's society. Communicating via social networks is easier than ever. Favorite social networking venues include:

- ○ Facebook
- ○ LinkedIn
- ○ Twitter
- ○ YouTube
- ○ Pinterest
- ○ Instagram

Create Networking Referral Lists

Referral lists are made up of contacts in your network. If you feel comfortable referring your contacts to others, he or she should be added to your referral list. The contacts on your referral list will be linked somehow to your field or area of expertise. As you refer others to the contacts on your referral list, it will affect your reputation. Therefore, it's imperative to consider beforehand the people and types of contacts you wish to include.

Develop Interpersonal Relationships

Networking, when done well, leads to lasting relationships. While networking can, and often does, require significant energy to transform a simple meeting into a relationship, it is well worth the time and effort. Through careful action, trustworthiness, and maintaining boundaries, casual exchanges can blossom into meaningful connections over time.

Careful and Specific Actions

Some people feel that networking is about social manipulation and is, therefore, insincere. However, sincerity comes through when you are about helping others and, in turn, helping yourself as well. While you certainly don't need to add every single person you come across to your professional network, you can always be genuine in your interactions, even when being specific about who to pursue. Choose connections with those whom you share interests, passions, or goals. In doing this, you allow these commonalities to create the root of the relationship. By addressing your interests, goals, and passions when first meeting people, you'll be able to identify potential contacts and like-minded individuals quickly.

Trustworthiness

It can be difficult to trust people you've never met before. Likewise, it might be difficult for them to trust you as well. However, when you keep your word, starting with following up when you say you will, people quickly learn that they can trust you. Practicing what you preach will help boost your reputation and increase the chances your contacts will want to do business with you and continue the relationship. In addition to following up in a timely fashion, make sure to be punctual for meetings and phone calls, commit what you can do, and make promises that you can follow through on. These actions will help others see you as trustworthy.

Maintain Boundaries

Boundaries can be difficult to manage when blending the personal and professional, but it is imperative for your sanity and well-being that you maintain them. If you fail to establish boundaries and enforce them, then your relationships become intrusive or overbearing. In addition to establishing and enforcing your boundaries, you need to respect the constraints of others. Everyone has different boundaries because we all have different needs. When deciding your boundaries, consider the following:

- When would I like to be contacted? Responded to?
- What time(s) in my schedule are "me" time?
- When is it okay to say "no"?
- How can I communicate these boundaries to my contacts? For example, state that you understand the importance of the meeting. However, you have to submit your book this week. You are open for a 15-minute phone conversation or meet them next week.
- How can I handle people who violate my boundaries?

Investing in Relationships

Building relationships take time and energy. If you desire for a contact to become a more meaningful connection, you need to reach out to the person. Send an e-mail, give someone a phone call, or message your contact via text or social media. Build time into your day to conduct these communications. A person is more likely to form a relationship with you if he or she is made to feel important. Take time out to show people how important they are and support them to succeed and you'll form real relationships instead of just having a few connections.

Engaging in Dialogue

Communication and listening are both integral to creating connections, but so is dialogue. Dialogue differs a bit from simple communication because the dialogue is a two-way, back-and-forth method of communication that enhances understanding and builds relationships. Successful dialogue incorporates active listening and respectful responses, even if you disagree with someone.

Steps to Dialogue:

○ Listen attentively.
○ Speak after the other person has completed their sentence.
○ Be respectful and polite, even if you disagree.
○ Pause and reflect before you present your case.

Allow Relationships to Develop Naturally

All relationships develop naturally within their timeframe. While it is imperative to follow-up with contacts, you don't want to appear clingy or desperate. If someone does not wish to develop a relationship with you, respect that person's desire and spend your energy elsewhere. As a rule, it is appropriate to reach out three times. If you have received no response by your third attempt, you have an answer regarding the person's desire to connect.

When following up with others, use common sense and your comfort level as your guides. How frequently would you expect someone to contact you? How much contact would you consider overbearing?

Common Networking Mistakes

We're all busy individuals, and it's very easy to let things slide sometimes. However, when it comes to networking, we need to be at our best in order to avoid a few common mistakes. Unequal giving and taking, believing false expectations and assumptions, setting unattainable goals, and overreliance on networking tools are all standard errors when beginning to network.

Unequal Give and Take

When forming a new professional relationship, it's important to show how you're an asset to the other party. You need to offer some value and give the person a reason to continue the communication and connection. If the individual feels used from the beginning, he or she will not want to continue the relationship. It is important to give before taking when establishing a relationship with someone new.

When giving, you don't have to be over-the-top. Simply providing a referral or even advice (assuming it's solicited) can count as giving. Once you have given, the relationship of give-and-take has begun.

Not Following Up

While networking is certainly about making new connections, it's also necessary to follow up to deepen those connections. It can be exciting to meet so many new people that it can be easy to forget to follow-up. It's also necessary to follow-up individually with people in order to show them they're important. Finally, following up in a timely manner is also crucial, because this conveys to the contact that you want to pursue a connection and build a relationship. Failing to communicate with a person in a timely fashion could cause him or her to forget your conversation or cause him or her to think you don't want a connection

Believing False Expectations and Assumptions

People develop or hold expectations of others often without even realizing it. One frequent example of this is assuming that others should automatically want to help you or care about your needs. Believing these false expectations sets you up for disappointment and sets others up for failure. While it can be difficult not to get your hopes up, it's best to operate without expectations until someone tells you clearly what they can do. Also, don't automatically make assumptions about your contacts based on their outward appearances or mannerisms.

Setting Unattainable Goals

Another common error is setting goals that are unattainable in regards to networking. While it's great to set goals for networking, assuming you'll meet Bill Gates next week is unrealistic. As is frequently the case with life, you often have to work your way up the chain of command when networking. Assuming you're going to meet many useful contacts in a short amount of time is also relatively lofty. It takes time to establish genuine connections and build relationships. You must take into consideration that at some networking affairs, you may not meet anyone who can help you. It's important to keep your goals realistic in order to stay motivated. If you set your goals too high and then fail to meet them, you might become discouraged and stop networking altogether.

Overreliance on Networking Tools

Earlier we discussed networking tools, such as blogs and social media. Even structured networking events can be considered to be networking tools. While these tools can help you meet new contacts, overreliance on these tools can make you lazy and cause your actual network to dwindle. While meeting new contacts is great, tools can't put in the effort to follow up with contacts or communicate with them— these are things that you must do. Also, while online resources are great to utilize, they are no substitute for meeting people in person. The tools are only as useful as the person wielding them; make the effort so that the tools can work for you.

Time Management

Networking takes time and because of this, sometimes time management can become an issue. When developing your schedule, build in time for networking. Make sure to prioritize. For example, it's more important to follow-up with a new contact than to have lunch with someone you just dined with two days ago. Additionally, make it easier on yourself by connecting online when possible or organizing a group activity for several contacts.

Prioritize Contacts

Once you have a list of contacts, it's important to prioritize them. Not everyone will be interested in pursuing a relationship with you, and some individuals may be more helpful to you than others. Prioritization is key to help you hone in on contacts who are most likely to become close. Once you have developed your list of contacts, narrow it down by

- Individuals with similar values and vision
- Individuals with useful knowledge
- Individuals with beneficial contacts
- Individuals who seem interested in pursuing a connection

The more criteria each contact meets, the higher his or her priority is to you. For example, if someone has several beneficial contacts and a wealth of knowledge, that person would take precedence over someone you met at a party who knows no one in your field. Rearrange your list with the highest priority contacts at the top and work your way down.

Organize Group Activities

Creating group activities for several contacts to participate in serves several purposes that benefit network management. It helps you connect with many contacts in person at the same time. It also allows your contacts to meet one another. Keep the group activities enjoyable for everyone and informal. Some of these activities could include:

- Dining
- Bowling/Billiards
- Local readings or community events
- Art walk
- Live theater or musical performances
- Sports games

Connect Online

It's imperative to engage online regularly in order to maintain the interest of your contacts. Frequently updating your status, blog, etc. is necessary. Also, you can't just wait for the comments to come to you; you must also comment on others' blogs or profile information in order to stay visible and engaged.

Schedule Your Network Activities

To keep networking a priority and to not overbook yourself, it's best to keep a schedule. It's often best to plan your schedule a week or so in advance and then adjust as situations arise. Make sure that you're leaving time for group activities, updating online communications, and private meetings with contacts. Having a schedule will help keep you on track and less likely to neglect your networking responsibilities.

Manage Personal and Professional Networks

It's not enough to just create professional networks; you also must manage and maintain them. Staying in contact with those you connect with, giving resources to your contacts, and setting healthy boundaries are all important parts of managing your network. It's also important to quickly respond when someone reaches out to you.

Finally, while it can seem difficult, separating your personal life from your professional life will also help your network to thrive. While people are drawn to those with similar hobbies and interests, it's best to keep the ins and outs of your personal life private. Being circumspect will ensure that your network sees you as the trusted professional that you truly are.

Respond Quickly

Responding to your contacts in a timely fashion shows that you value them and their time. When you ignore someone, it may give the impression that you are not interested in that individual and are unhelpful. If you are busy, you may respond with a short email. If this is the case, schedule a meeting with the person so that you can follow up later. Above all, responding to your contacts is the most important thing you can do to build your network.

Give Often

Networks are created so that people can help one another. Part of this helping is giving. Earlier, we talked about giving first before asking for help. It's also helpful to find a way to help when a contact asks you to. Occasionally you might not be able to, but if this is the case, try to connect him or her with someone who can help.

Separate Personal and Business Activities

No one likes a business-all-the-time robot, and it's true that connections are often formed based on similar areas of interest. However, to keep your professional image intact, it's best not to integrate your personal and professional lives. Setting boundaries for personal and professional activities will make life less complicated for you in the end and make it easier to network professionally.

Some ways to separate the personal and professional include having both personal and professional social media profiles. Also, privacy settings on your personal page can limit what certain people can see. Having one e-mail address for business and another for personal activities can also help keep you organized (as long as you frequently check both).

Stay Physically In-touch

It's easy to stay connected with phone calls or the internet. However, making a connection physically often lends a personal touch. You can accomplish this if your contacts are local. However, even if your contacts live in other areas, it is still possible to connect in person. While it does take more effort to travel, sometimes you may be near contacts without realizing it. When making your list of contacts, include the city (and state or province) in which each contact resides. The next time you book a flight, see if there are any layovers in the contact's city. Also, when traveling to conferences or other business opportunities, check your list to see who is nearby. Your contacts will certainly appreciate the extra effort!

Final Thoughts

- Carl Jung: The meeting of two personalities is like the contact of two chemical substances: if there is any reaction, both are transformed.
- Dale Carnegie: When dealing with people, remember you are not dealing with creatures of logic, but creatures of emotion.
- Confucius: What you do not want done to yourself, do not do to others.
- Maya Angelou: I've learned that people will forget what you said, people will forget what you did, but people will never forget how you made them feel.
- Tennessee Williams: Life is partly what we make it, and partly what it is made by the friends we choose.
- Deepak Chopra: Giving connects two people, the giver and the receiver, and this connection gives birth to a new sense of belonging.

CHAPTER 6

KNOWING YOUR MARKET

Build your brand, live it, and over-deliver on promises to sustain your brand over time. If your brand makes a mistake, take the responsibility to repair and restore it.

Divya Parekh

A car pulled up to the curb and Dee got out of the back seat. Once again, I marveled how spry she was for her age. I walked over from the entrance of the restaurant to escort her inside. She took my arm and said, "This is kind of you, Sally. I appreciate the invitation to lunch."

Once inside, the maître de took us to a quiet table overlooking the bay. As we got comfortable, I said, "This is a small token of my appreciation for what you have done for me. I believe your material on relationships is dead on. I am definitely including it in my book."

"I am so happy you are doing that, Sally. Also, I am gratified you liked it so much."

"It has been a big help to me already. Besides, this lunch is more than that. Over the past six months of your mentoring, I have seen a tremendous change in my approach to business and life, and it has been paying off. Your coaching has been invaluable to me. I have accomplished my short-term goals as I continue working on my long-term goals. I have more clients, improved revenues, and I am clear on how I want to expand my business to the next level."

"That's excellent, dear. Your self-assurance about your career is thanks enough." Her eyes danced as she looked around the dining room. "However, I would never turn down a nice lunch with a terrific friend."

I laughed and blushed a little. After we had ordered, I said, "You sent me a note last week after I invited you to lunch, coaching me to start thinking about my market. You said my relationship to market was the next topic we were going to cover."

Dee took a sip of her white wine before answering. "Yes, Sally, the relationship with market is the next logical subject in our progression of topics. While we all think we know who our market is before we start our companies, spending time in our day-to-day work will help us define our market. Once we do that, we can then customize and tailor our efforts to that market."

"It's funny that you mention that," I said. "For the most part, I have remarkable energy for my clients. I love the ones that take my coaching and run with it. They are always eager to implement the ideas and strategies we discuss. In their success lies my success. It is very gratifying."

"Why do you love only some clients?" asked Dee.

For a minute, I had to think about how to phrase my response. "Well," I answered sheepishly. "There are those who suck the energy out of me like a huge sponge. They complain about spending their money because they do not see substantial results. I am experiencing frustration because I devote my time and focus equally to all of my clients. However, I'm not getting anywhere with all of them. I'll be honest. It's hard to love the negative people who don't value what I have to offer them."

"Sally, your success is directly related to your knowledge and understanding of your clients. In business, it is important to focus on growing one type of crop so that your harvest is great. To do that, you need to prune the weeds so that your ideal clients blossom. In other words, if you provide services to your ideal client, your clients will experience phenomenal success. As a result, you will be more successful in achieving personal and business goals. You will eliminate the frustration of those who say you aren't helping them."

What is the Relationship with Market

Dee continued, "Usually, the underlying assumption is that an entrepreneur knows their business niche. It can focus on health, relationship, career, finance, business, weight loss...whatever. The relationship with your market is essential so you can be one with your market. That way, you can provide solutions for your clients in your particular area of expertise. Relationship with market is knowing and understanding your ideal client, establishing your brand, making a positive impact, and serving your clients to help them succeed in their personal, professional, and financial goals."

I took a minute to take this in while the waitress set our food in front of us. As the server left the table, I said, "That sounds like the first step of any business. I learned that in school. You have to know who your customers are."

"That's very true, Sally," said Dee. "However, the difference between ordinary and extraordinary business success is categorizing this concept into more specific components." She took one of the paper napkins on the table and fished a pen out of her pocketbook. She spent a couple of minutes writing before turning the napkin to me. "Here are the key points to have a successful relationship with market."

She had a list on the napkin that read:

- Knowing your ideal client.
- Understanding the transformation they desire.
- Know how to speak their language in your branding, your marketing, and your sales conversations, so as to provide them the answers to the provocative questions that keep them up at night.
- Your brand represents your promise of delivery to your clients.
- Your products and/or services enable your market to succeed.

Why Market Is Important to Business

Looking up from the napkin, I said, "So, the focus is on my ideal client?"

"That's right, Sally. Let me tell you about a client I had. Initially, this gentleman started out as a consultant providing services in several areas. He made decent money, but instead of focusing on his vision, he tried offering many services. This lack of attention caused his brand to become diluted. Therefore, he did not get the traction he needed to set his business apart from the crowd. Furthermore, his brand seemed to target multiple types of prospects instead of offering a real solution to a defined group. As a result, it was difficult for his ideal clients to resonate with his brand because his marketing message lacked solutions that would solve their problems. He was trying to appeal to many different people at the same time.

"There is no need to chase people," Dee continued. "Chasing people can turn the pleasure of what you do in business to pain. For this person, not only was running the business painful, he eventually went back to the corporate world to pay the bills while running his business on the side. If his approach had targeted only those whom he could indeed help with his expertise, he would have found enough clients to be a success.

"Marketing generates potential customers' interest in a business' products and services. In turn, this leads to the creation of a sales plan, communication with potential clients, and business development."

"Most companies have an entire department devoted to marketing," I said. "How do I compete with that?"

"We are not going to look at all aspects of marketing here," responded Dee. "Because so many options are available, the focus has shifted from selling to buying. In broad terms, a market can be diverse. However, if you want a sustainable business, the key is to narrow down your target market, which is your potential customers, to one particular segment of the market and provide them exactly what they want." Dee held up her hand as I was about to say something. "Let's take it one step further. Remove the word 'target' and replace it with a real person, your ideal client."

"So I should think about a client who I have helped overcome challenges?" I asked.

"Yes, that way your focus is on building a mutually beneficial long term relationship with that ideal client. The definition of an 'ideal client' is the one that you enjoy working with and who needs and seeks the emotional and financial transformation that you provide for their problems and challenges.

"Once you know and understand your clients, create value for them in your work. As you continue learning how your clients are evolving, your brand will adapt to serve your ideal clients while re-engineering the psychology of your business relationships. With that concept in mind, you are now using value-based entrepreneurship along with a trust-based relationship by exceeding the expectations of your customers, even in the face of pressure."

"So if I focus on my ideal client, I am going to increase my satisfaction rate with all of my clients right away," I exclaimed.

"Sally, in my experience, success is inherent when people resonate with each other. You know, different flowers may grow and thrive in different conditions. They all have diverse needs of soil, water, and sunlight. Not every plant can grow in the same circumstances. Likewise, you are not going to foster growth in every client, unless you work with clients who can thrive with your efforts."

"I never quite thought of my market in such specific terms," I said. "I need to create a strategic plan to build the relationship with my market. How would you recommend going about it, Dee?"

Dee gave me a reassuring smile. "You have nailed down exactly what a relationship with market needs to be – built on the foundation of a plan. As to how to go about it…" At this point, Dee went back in her purse and pulled out a flash drive. Handing it to me she said, "I put some essential techniques on this flash drive for you to consider. You've grasped the concept of relationship with market. With this, you will find ways to implement it more fully for your business." She chuckled. "And for all the businesses you will have in the future."

"You certainly have confidence in me."

"You've shown me how well you take what I share and make it happen in your entrepreneur efforts," said Dee. "The only way you can make me think that this relationship with market will not work for you is if we can't order dessert after this terrific lunch!"

We laughed together and spent the rest of our time reviewing what I thought made up my best clients. Yes, we did have dessert. After Dee left, I went back to my office and plugged in the flash drive. Here is a synopsis of what I learned in having a successful relationship with market.

How to Strengthen Your Relationship with Your Market

If you want your business to grow exponentially, it is important to recognize that you have to bridge the gap where your business is and where you want it to be. You need a well-conceived marketing plan and execution strategy to close the gap. Your products and/or services will bring the solution that your ideal clients need. In turn, you will move forward on your path to success.

As you grow your business, you will no longer have to start from scratch. You will be building on the success of your current projects. The success of your business today and tomorrow is driven by client experience and doing the right things for the right reasons, and not because they are paying you.

When you have developed a genuine relationship with your client, you authentically provide them the experience they desire. The customized service allows you to stand out in the crowd. As you share your expertise while serving your ideal clients, they realize that you are the one for them. Gradually, they become champions for your business, spreading the word to others about your great products and services.

As you develop a strong and continuously adaptive relationship with your market, it allows you to:

- Attain an in-depth knowledge about your ideal client
- Know and establish your brand (narrowing your focus).
- Develop a focused marketing message for your ideal client.
- Connect with the ideal client with your focused marketing message.
- Create the transformation for your client and provide them the experience they desire.
- Create cheerleaders who support your growth because they want others to succeed as well.

When establishing a new contact, it is important to remember the principles from the interlude chapter on relationship building. For the sake of this section, we will consider that the contact is a potential client. As you continue to grow your business successfully, referrals from friends and family, social networking, and community events might not be enough to grow your business. Defining your ideal client, positioning your brand to codify the value your brand offers, and delivering your promise is imperative to business success.

Define Your Ideal Client

Let your values guide you in determining the ideal client with whom you are going to build relationships. You design your business model in such a manner that it allows you to work with people who value your services. Knowing your ideal clients allows you to dive deep into your services or products and develop a unique branding promise that offers your clients the transformation they require.

As a starting point in developing your ideal client's profile, select one paid or unpaid client who is your favorite. (Henceforth, we will refer to your ideal client as 'avatar.') Bestow your favorite client avatar with a nickname. An ideal avatar is a person that you can provide a solution to that will overcome the problem or challenge they are facing. Working with you enables them to transform into who they want to become and achieve their desired goals.

You have to ask questions to understand and know your avatar. These questions address demographics, psychographics, and behavioral attributes of the client.

- The first step is to collect the demographic information of the client. Some of the common characteristics include age or age range, gender, education level, income level, nationality, family information, geographical location, industry, organization, functional role, and other relevant information. You may not need all of the characteristics, or you may have other characteristics that you want to add to describe your avatar. It is also important to keep a pulse on how your demographic trend is changing.
- The psychographic information includes their values, interests, preferences, opinions, hobbies, affiliations, lifestyle, attitudes, personality, etc.
- The behavioral information takes a deep dive into your avatar's life. You come to know their burning desires, dreams, rants, and frustrations that keep them awake at night. You discover the personal and career goals they want to reach, what's most important to them, the risks they want to reduce or eliminate, and their sense of urgency. You want to understand their decision criteria so you can better serve them.

One of the elements to keep in mind is that they want more than your product and/or services. They are looking for recognition, respect, service that provides a unique experience, reliability, and friendship. We care about these aspects as human beings. It is important to remember that you are dealing with people here, not some soulless object.

When you merge the hard data of demographics and soft data of psychographics and behavioral information, you begin to develop a broader, more expansive and in-depth picture of who they are. You understand their wants, needs, aspirations, and goals. This knowledge becomes the fertile ground for the tree of branding to grow and provides the fruits of positive impact and success to the client through your product and/or services. The very fact that your products and/or services are entirely client-focused will make you stand apart.

As an authentic business provider, you will know and respect your clients. Authenticity causes you, your team, and your brand to broadcast the message that you care and what you do focuses on your clients' needs. Your intentions align with your actions and bring transparency to your interaction with them as you keep moral and ethical considerations in sight at all times. Ultimately, the goal is to help them succeed at every turn.

Branding and You

You want to create an authentic message for your ideal client or target market.

The rapid changes in the way people do business may seem difficult to embrace. However, plenty of companies have navigated these changing seas successfully. Your branding is the start of building your relationship with your market.

Branding is an assurance that a person, product or service possesses sustaining qualities, benefits, and distinctions from peers and competitors. It is the bridge that joins your passions, personality, and assets with your intention. It is what you provide to the person you want to influence. Branding is the guarantee that you will deliver what you promise; your product and service will do what you say about it consistently.

By branding, you convince the customer of your intentions without asking them to buy products or services. It is effective if the customer perceives your service or product to be the best in the market. Branding is the trust consumers have for businesses, personal products, or services. An active and influential brand promises an extremely positive experience to your customer when they hire or buy from you. It builds an expectation that you will deliver what you promise.

Your brand sets you apart from others based on the expectation created from a customer's perspective. The brand allows you to market your product or services to your avatar because they resonate with your message, and they seek the experience and transformation your brand offers. Ensure that you develop a strategy to bridge the gap between where you are and where you want to be. Your brand needs to show up authentically on a consistent basis so that you build a trust with your ideal client that will never break.

Defining Your Brand

Establishing your brand can be discomforting, time-laborious, and tough at times. Creating a strategy to identify your brand is critical because your brand is not about what you are. Rather it is who you are, what your beliefs and values are, and what value you provide to your target market. Factor in who you are today and how others will know you in twenty-five years. In some cases, it may line up smoothly, or you might have a gap between the two that you need to bridge. The strategy you utilize will help you define, develop, promote, and sustain your brand.

First, decide if you are going to brand the company, product/service, or an individual. Secondly, it is important to understand and define the vision, mission, and goals of what you are branding. Since you have done your homework regarding your avatar, it will be easier to create a unique selling proposition - offering solutions specific to your ideal client. Defining your brand also includes the perception of your future and existing clients about your company or brand regarding your quality, characteristics, image, etc. Additionally, the focus is heavy on benefits, promises, and outstanding features of your products and services.

Develop Your Brand

The name, logo, and tagline of your brand serve as the trademark and should be able to generate the image of your brand in an avatar's mind. Your tagline is the indicator of what your brand is about. The launch of your brand tells your market about what your brand stands for. Managing and nurturing the brand to maturity requires consistency and the grit to adapt to the market in the face of changes.

Examples of nurturing the brand involve providing personalized experiences to the client. To accomplish this, engage them through conversations, surveys, quizzes, and then continue adding to the value that you provide to your avatar. As you do this and test the market, you are taking a risk. You might find that you are failing in certain aspects of your branding efforts. Remember that failing helps you learn, grow, stretch, adapt and work on providing what your client is seeking.

Promoting your brand involves an intentional awareness of building on social media and linking with decision makers, connectors, and knowledge hubs. Social media serves as a global market place providing you an extensive outreach. Decision makers can work with you and promote you, connectors can connect you with the right people for your brand, and knowledge hubs can share the industry trends with you. Once you promote your brand, it is important to sustain the brand through interaction, learning, and re-strategizing.

Delivering the Promise

You have identified your client, built your brand, and connected with your target market. Some of your target markets will become your clients, some might be on the fence, and others will not want your products or services. For your ideal clients, you should emphasize that you will not only meet their emotional and financial needs, but that the value you are providing is so remarkable that it will surpass their expectations as they achieve the success they desire. If you encounter failures, you learn and improve upon the value you deliver. It is important to stay in communication in real time with your ideal clients as well as your target market to get proper feedback.

Summation – Impact to Business

Build your relationships on the value of humanity and the foundation of caring for others' well-being. Do this so that interacting with you makes your ideal clients feel important and an integral part of your life.

Technology is changing today's world at light speed. Brands have emerged to influence every aspect of our life. Brands are used to find information (Bing, Google, Yahoo, etc.), share films (You Tube, Break, Metacafe), buy and sell products (EBay, Craigslist, Amazon), stay connected to others (Facebook, Myspace, Google chat), and gain knowledge (Wikipedia, TedTalks, HowStuffWorks).

A shift has occurred from the power of selling to the power of buying due to the presence of overwhelming choices and options. This shift gives the consumer the ability to choose. In the jungle of multimedia, a brand name represents the fulfillment of a promise made to your avatar, whether it is a product, service, or person. Personal branding gives you and your avatar the control in a world where change is constant. It allows you to define what you are going to deliver, whom you are going to work with, and by what rules you will play. When you correctly position your brand for your avatar, they know that you are their "go to" person.

When you review the strategies of successful people, products, and services, you find that success centers on specific and emotional concepts around the brand and these ideas strike a chord with the customers. A clear and meaningful identity sustains a brand, whether it is a person, product, or a service. Your brand relates to your avatar personally because association with an attractive, quality and successful brand provides you:

- A feeling of personal worth. (You deserve a Mercedes Benz because you only buy a car with quality engineering.)
- Validation of your beliefs and values, and thereby psychic satisfaction. (You give your business to people who believe what you believe. For example, you have stayed with your hairdresser because she is cheerful, gives an excellent haircut, and provides great customer service.)
- A product or service that serves you the best. (American Express is a good example of this. Their brand is a culture of service so that many consumers are willing to pay more for the privilege of using the card.)
- A sharp image of a successful person because successful people are using it. (Your VP reads books authored by Tony Robbins and so do you.)

- Help for day-to-day problems. The brand provides emotional satisfaction and financial benefits. (Samsung Galaxy Note 10.1 helps James Franco and other very busy people to organize every aspect of their lives.)
- Fulfillment of your needs. (Air France Airline has a reputation for comfort during air travel.)
- A sense of belonging because you are a part of the community comprised of like-minded people. (Star Trek fans mirror the actions of other fans and follow the crowd.)
- Reflection of how other people perceive you. (Cool people purchase iPhones.)
- People are more tolerant and forgiving of your mistakes (Athletes).

In summary, consumers are looking to connect with a person, product, or service. It is not just about what the product or service does. It is about why you do it. The "why" seeks the passion, vision, and mission underlying the product or service.

Branding forms the foundation of success in business. Branding will help you accept, adapt, and evolve with today's changing tide of technology. It is essential that your brand sustain its promise by over delivering the expected value consistently and providing the personalized transformational experience of success to your clients. It is important to be flexible, agile, and adaptive when change is constant. Our tomorrows need new and different actions and solutions today.

Life isn't about finding yourself. Life is about creating yourself. - George Bernhard Shaw.

Exercise to Manage Your Brand

As the owner of the brand, you represent your brand and have the need to be authentic both online and offline as you promote and market while hanging out with your ideal client. While maintaining the decorum of the situation, remain true to yourself as you participate in a conversation with your avatar to build a healthy relationship.

For example, if your brand stands for service, then it is important to strategize and execute the touchpoint client plan. The touchpoint plan considers the quality of customer experience during the interaction whether it is via email, social media, phone, opt-in page, free gifts, books, follow through, face to face, thank you emails and cards, newsletters, touching base, holiday greetings, and birthday acknowledgments. It is important that the quality of interaction is phenomenal and consistent at all touchpoints.

Ask these questions of your brand to determine its effectiveness:

1. Are your clients able to find you?

2. Are you building a community of like-minded individuals to foster connections, and ensure the opportunity for learning, growth, success and giving back to the community?

3. Are you filtering every action through this question, "Will this action serve my connections and clients to the best of my ability?" Maintain a log of each touchpoint (time, method, and quality of interaction as well as the market's response).

4. Are you showing up authentically in your communication whether it is online or offline?

5. Are you sharing your stories of struggles, successes, and challenges as they happen?

6. Are you serving as a leader to provide courage, connection, and value?

7. Are you going above and beyond what you promised to your client? For example, are you addressing the avatar by their names through the use of customer relationship management software, sending a personalized card or gifts, remembering the birthdays and holidays (www.sendoutcards.com/kindnessrules), sending bonuses or product discounts? Do you remember to send a simple 'thank you' when appropriate?

8. Are you compensating your clients for any canceled appointments or mistakes that have caused inconvenience through apologies and a gift that shows you care?

9. Do you celebrate their successes by recognizing them on social media or with a phone call or sending them a gift card or gifts?

10. Are you asking for real time feedback about your product or services?

11. Are you keeping a pulse on their changing needs and emerging problems so that you can provide a solution?

12. Are you adapting your product or service to meet the shifting trends and needs?

13. Are your clients talking about your remarkable product or service to others?

CHAPTER 7

THE POWER OF TEAMWORK

Individually, we are one drop. Together, we are an ocean.

Ryunosuke Satoro

Walking up to Dee's house, I hear my name over the low roll of the surf. Shielding the sun from my eyes, I see Dee on the edge of the water waving to me. I jog over to her and give her a hug when we meet up.

"Thank you, dear," said Dee. "You seem extra happy today!"

"I am. Ever since we had lunch together, I have been applying what you showed me about the relationship with my market. I have to say that the new clients I have been mentoring are more receptive to the coaching I am providing. Also, I have learned how to gently release clients who are not yet ready to be coached. Recently a client, Dawn, with whom I did not seem to be connecting with very well, sat down with me at my request. I was very open with Dawn that we were not progressing as expected. Through our conversation, I learned that Dawn was taking care of sick parents, and it was taking more of her time than she anticipated. We decided to put our work on hiatus until she is ready to get back into it. Now, both of us are at peace with the outcome."

"I'm not surprised that you have taken to the relationship with market so well," Dee responded. "You knew the basics of it. I think you only needed some clarification on how important it is to steer your company in the right direction."

"Everything you have helped me with has been right on point," I said. "I know I have said it before…but thank you."

"I appreciate that," she said with a big smile. "Remember to share all of this with others when you get the chance."

"The book is certainly coming along," I said. "I think you will like the finished product. So, what are we going to talk about today?"

"You mentioned when we were last together that you started hiring some people. I think this is the proper time to discuss your relationship with team."

I laughed. "You must be spying on me. While it is great to be able to start hiring, I am finding that it also has its challenges."

"Everything that has to do with dealing with people has its issues," said Dee. "Especially when you are paying them to do work for you. Tell me what's going on."

The Relationship with Team

Waiting until the sound of a crashing wave passed, I began to relate my hiring experiences to Dee.

"I now have a couple of employees. One employee has worked out fabulously. She took ownership of her job and hit the ground running. The other one needs constant direction and supervision. It surprised me, because based on his qualifications and what we discussed in the interview; I thought he would have no trouble working independently."

Dee walked in silence for a few minutes. I saw that she was thinking. I kept quiet until she said, "Sally, hiring is one of the key elements of building a team."

"I never thought of the three of us as a team," I said.

"It doesn't matter. As soon as you have two or more people, you have a team. With a team, the leader becomes the catalyst that leads his or her team to thrive, so each member is providing extreme value both individually and collectively. You are that leader, Sally. When you strengthen the relationship among the team, you are fortifying the plant of today to grow into a tree of solutions tomorrow. When you have a weak link with a member of your team, you need to see what changes you can implement to strengthen those relationships."

"So this relationship with team applies to anyone I do anything with as the owner of my company?" I inquired.

Shaking her head slowly, Dee said. "Here I am specifically talking about employees or contractors you have on your payroll." She smiled again. "Spoiler alert here. The next relationship we will talk about has to do with partners, including those you work with in various capacities for mutual benefiting outcomes. Today, we talk about people who are part of your company."

"Where do we begin?" I ask.

"Do you have your notebook with you?"

"Better than a notebook," I said, fishing my cell phone out of my shoulder bag and holding it in the air. "We can record what you say as we walk."

"Great! These are questions any team leader needs to ask themselves," Dee continued as I held the phone close to her.

I am sharing what I recorded:

Questions for Team Leader

1. Are you committed to your team's success?

2. Do you have a team of full-time employees or independent contractors or a mix?

3. Does your team know the purpose or mission of your organization?

4. Are they aligned with that purpose and mission?

5. Do you have the right systems and processes in place that allows your team members to excel?

6. Do you have the right team members who share your values and are ready to learn their responsibilities and take on a leadership role when needed?

7. Are your team members clear about your expectations?

8. Are you clear about their expectations?

9. Do you have a fearless culture that promotes participation? For example, a freedom to ask questions?

10. Are people willing to have open discussions and express their opinions without the fear of repercussions?

11. Do you and your team members trust each other?

12. Do people take pride in their work and work for the client's transformation?

13. Do members train cross functionally, step into different roles, and perform various functions as needed?

14. Do members make effective decisions to ensure excellent quality of products or services while maintaining high productivity?

15. Do members feel valued for their contribution to the team?

16. Do you have repeat customers and do you get referrals from your clients?

When Dee finished, I exclaimed, "Wow, that's a lot to consider."

Dee gave a throaty chuckle. "I said entrepreneurship could be fun; I didn't say it wouldn't take work. Remember that business is a system in which all parts and processes contribute to the success or failure of the whole. The business involves the building of a team, having it function well together, and providing what they need to sustain them."

"I am beginning to realize that," I sighed. "There is a lot I still have to think about and put into place.

"Yes, that's right, Sally. As soon as you get past the one-woman show stage of your company, there are other factors you have to start incorporating into the business operations. With a team, you have to ensure that they understand your expectation of continuous improvement in your business and the company culture. The relationship to team involves learning the tactical means to create that team. This includes organizational planning, hiring, and training them. To do this properly, you have to understand your role as their leader in motivating, removing barriers, and providing the right amount of knowledge and support for them to grow into their greatest potential. You want them working towards a common goal. What you are doing is building an interdependent community of independent, committed, accountable individuals with different skills and inspiring them to work together towards the shared vision, mission, and goals that you establish."

It sounded overwhelming. "Although I know some of that, I guess I never thought about breaking it down in such detail."

"We never do until we are in the middle of it," said Dee. She suddenly stopped in the sand, snapped her fingers, and turned to me. "I have an idea. Can you arrange your schedule to be free next Tuesday?"

I quickly pulled out my phone again and checked my schedule. "Sure. What do you have in mind?"

"On that day, I am visiting one of my companies. I'm not involved in the day-to-day activities, but my people like to see me once in a while. This place has an exceptional team. I want you to come along with me. It would be a pleasure to introduce you. You are welcome to go around and pick the brains of my managers and staff about what makes a good team. Some of them you saw at my party when we first met. Usually, seeing a good example is worth thousands of words. What do you think?"

Dee gleaned the answer by my smile. "I'm all for it. I want to get a handle on the relationship with my team before I hire more people."

As we walked back, Dee continued talking about the relationship with team as I recorded her. For the remainder of this chapter, I reference what I learned from that recording, as well as my experience during the visit to her client's company.

It was evident that her client's team worked well together. It felt like I was in a well-oiled machine without sacrificing the personalities of anybody working there. Here is the rest of what I learned about this significant relationship.

Why Team Is Important to Business

Today's entrepreneurs experience challenges of maintaining value-driven leadership in the face of constant pressure, changing technology, changing trends, and shifting customer preferences. Also, when a company faces rapid growth, it encounters greater challenges of operating effectively while striving to deliver high-quality products and services to their customers and clients. At that point, the company has to be able to compete with competitors on price. The growth phase creates high-stress levels due to a bigger workload, doing more with less, rapid hiring, keeping team members fulfilled, and still maintaining the entrepreneurial passion and innovation that a young business has.

Several processes can bring solutions to these challenges. However, the focus here is on the issues related to developing the team of employees and/or contractors who are involved in the operations of the company. It is important to realize that while the entire company is considered a team, there are many smaller teams involved that make up the whole. A team could include any number of arrangements. A few examples include the full-time employees that you work with daily; employees who operate parts of the company that you have little to do with; or an independent contractor that you work with through the Internet or remote access. You might have teams that concentrate on human resources, overall management, or in direct service to clients. You can bring on team members by hiring directly, using temporary agencies, outsourcing the job, or teaming up with independent contractors.

As the head of your organization, you need to make sure the smaller teams function well, and that they relate together to further the mission of the business.

Successful businesses or organizations realize that people are their biggest asset. Becoming excellent at developing this relationship skill will go a long way to meeting your goals as the head of the company.

Attitudes are contagious. A negative attitude can create a downward spiral within the team, or a positive attitude can uplift the team even in the hardest times. When teams do not work together, it affects the entire organization negatively by lowering revenues, morale and creating a negative culture. As a result, it affects innovation, productivity, and the profitability of the business or an organization. Attitude leads to success or failure. Studies have shown that people matter, culture matters, and results matter in the workplace.

When you develop teams based on humanistic values focusing on purpose, encouragement, real-time feedback, and reinforcing structures, they excel. Happy team members play a significant role in each other's personal, professional, and financial success because they help achieve the company's goals. When you work as a team, everybody is involved in some way in the planning, designing, developing, and implementing of those goals. When you achieve the goals, the entire team cheers and celebrates. After all, they were highly involved in making it happen!

When you have a connected team, you experience the contributions and support that enables you to orchestrate productivity, innovation, creativity, and the best quality of products and services. This profitability enhances everyone's life. Your business becomes more than a paycheck to your team or something that sucks the joy out of people's lives.

When a team is clicking together on all cylinders, there is increased customer satisfaction and greater employee satisfaction with lower staff turnover. The company experiences higher productivity, greater quality products and services, more significant sales, and greater profitability,

A flower grows strong when all the parts of the plant work together to achieve one thing – healthy growth. Similarly, when everyone in the business is attuned to each other and working for the greater good, then spectacular business acceleration and sustainable success are the results.

How to Strengthen Your Relationship with Your Team

The entrepreneur's job is to lead, inspire, and encourage the employees or contractors. It also includes the responsibility for hiring, firing, assessing, and improving people's performance. As a company grows, a Human Relations Team can take on these tasks. Although these functions are divergent, a successful leader can converge both the positive and negative aspects of these services to create a positive, high performing, and highly productive work team. While you build your team, remember and apply the principles from the interlude chapter about interactions with people. Active teams necessitate people to collaborate efficiently.

When you are starting out, you establish reliable systems, maintain them, and continually ask whether these systems need improvement. It is important to have clearly defined and easy to understand processes that use the systems. These processes reduce ambiguity in your people who use them.

The next step is hiring the right people and bringing out the best in them. As a self-evaluation, you have to ask yourself regularly if you have the correct people on the team. Once you have the right systems, processes, and people, it is possible to build tough teams that are adaptive to changing environments and dynamics that can deliver in the face of pressure.

Processes and Systems

A process is a series of structured events or activities to help you complete a task or project whereas a system is the "what" that is used to implement the process. For example, let's look at the process of coaching an employee. Let's say a leader coaches a new team member. First, you need to be open-minded about what you are going to accomplish together. Then, you have a conversation with the team member and set goals jointly for him or her. Next, you brainstorm together to create a roadmap for achieving the goals with milestones to track the progress. Throughout the goal achievement process, you exchange real-time feedback ensuring that the employee has access to resources and inspiration essential to achieve the goals.

An example of a system could be the use of Microsoft Project to create a project timeline and an online feedback system to document the progress and exchange information.

When the processes and systems are complex, you may observe team members putting the task off for later and sometimes leaving the job incomplete. On the other hand, efficient systems allow you to improve the process. When the business systems and processes as a whole are simplified, you observe that you reduce or even eliminate the requirement of subject matter experts and oversight controls. The simplicity, in turn, empowers the team members to become leaders who can use their time, energy, and passion to do the right things rather than normal stuff bogging them down.

Hiring the Right People

In a start-up or relatively new business, job requirements for employees may vary depending on what is critical to the business. It becomes imperative to success that you have leaders throughout the organization who are willing to recognize the norms, highs, and lows of the business. They should possess the quality to adapt, adjust, take ownership of a situation, and push the project or work through to achieve the goals.

As leaders step up, they leverage others' strengths and bring out the best in them. Besides having the right technical and functional knowledge for their position, the people you choose should also have the interpersonal and emotional management skills to be viable and fruitful. Hence, hiring the right people becomes a critical factor in business success. Hiring them requires resources, money, time and effort. It is similar to preparing the soil for seeding. It takes time, but the fruits your efforts bear in the future are worth the wait.

How you hire people is significant in finding the best people for *your* organization. Behavior-based questions and personality assessments provide insight into a person's talents. Listen for the responses that indicate the habitual use of a talent. Additionally, asking a candidate what brings satisfaction to them demonstrates the areas of their strengths and fulfillment. If feasible, meet the final candidate in three different environments (for example, going for a nature walk, meeting for coffee, inviting them to a team meeting) to get the full picture of who they are. When you match the right talents with the right job, you see the right results.

As the company's leader, you have to step into the role of a coach looking to work jointly with team members to unleash their potential. You might want to hire another employee like an existing excellent staff member. You know the type of person who works well in your company. You will lose good people because they want to move on to something different or better, so prepare for such an event by having a profile of the kind of person that fits best with your team. The talent profile will help you to hire the right people consistently. By hiring the best people and working with them, you know how you can use their strengths in a team setting.

Bringing out the Best

After you hire the right person, leaders help those team members be more, do more, and achieve more by focusing on their strengths while managing their shortcomings. It is about being realistically positive, instilling confidence in team members, and celebrating every win. When team members know that job duties might vary depending on what is critical to business, then they are excited about new opportunities, learning, and growing. Flexibility, agility, and adaptability becomes an essential ingredient for the growth of business where people cross-train functionally and can step in as a leader when needed. They know how to take ownership and lead the team to successful project completion or situation handling.

Be sure you bring on team members from diverse backgrounds and varied personalities so that your members bring different perspectives to the company. Hire people who accept responsibility and provide a good balance of skills, abilities, and career aspirations. Match the right team with the right work for successful action plan implementation and project completion.

Various Phases of Teams

Teams go through different phases of development. In the initial phase, team members become familiar with the organization's purpose, vision, mission, and values. They then determine overall objectives, set goals based on the objectives, create an action plan, and implement the action plan. During the implementation, they evaluate the process, performance, wins, and deficiencies. You can then adapt your plan accordingly. However, recognize that any change execution will experience resistance. A change of responsibilities, members, or organization might require established teams to revisit and re-clarify their roles, mission, and process.

As a leader, you ensure that roles and responsibilities for the team and its members are clearly defined and understood by everyone. Leaders take on the role of a coach who guides the team members through the inevitable changes that occur.

Setting Objectives and Goals

Team members set mutually agreed clear objectives (overall targets of teams leading to an action plan) and goals (specific tasks to be performed to achieve the mission) using SMART (Specific, Measurable, Attainable, Relevant, Time-bound) metrics for both the process and desired outcomes. Communication between team members and leaders promotes clarity about the goals and knowledge about how to guide their efforts for goal achievement.

Everyone on the team needs to know that they have a voice in determining how the team will work since they have a stake in the emotional and financial outcomes. Team members need to understand the consequences of failures that an organization will face from a dissonant team that performs poorly due to self-serving intentions as well as the impact on customer satisfaction, emotional benefits, financial profits, and sustainable success. At this juncture, alignment of personal and organizational vision, mission, and values give a sense of direction, clarity, and drive for productivity.

It is your business so have an open conversation about the shared purpose/vision and goal trajectory of the team with team members. Ensure that everyone is clear on their individual and collective goals and the direction of efforts. As a team leader, build a sufficient knowledge database of information relevant to the achievement of your team's goals. A successful team usually exhibits a high level of personal respect shared by all members. Members promote an environment of trust, candor and open communication in which each person can contribute, question and express their concerns.

Members understand that great relationships begin with an understanding of diversity, creating a safe and supportive environment where trust grows, and risk-taking is allowed. Develop a co-coaching approach between members, using humor to de-stress a tense situation and advocating mutual respect, positive reinforcement, and real-time feedback.

Success principles are action-guiding principles that direct how interactions, work, and communication occur in your team. As a leader, you open the floor to team members to jointly create and agree upon team success principles and an action plan to achieve the goals.

While picking the brains of Dee's team, I came up with measures and questions to get the members of a team thinking in order to come up with success principles and an action plan.

Crafting the Team Success Principles and Action Plan: Role of members:

- Clarify what each member brings to the team; understand and know the significance of the contribution of each member.

- How does the dynamics of connectivity and interdependence of different roles and responsibilities play out?

Team communication:

- How can we have a commitment from every member for team success?
- What are the preferred methods of communication amongst team members?
- How can we build an environment of trust, support, and safety within the team?
- How can we foster good relationships between team members?
- How do we have healthy discussions over conflicts?
- Once the members are past healthy conflicts, how can they focus on building a positive team environment?
- How can we bring innovative and creative ideas to the table?
- How can the team be both value-driven and result-driven?
- How do we learn from each other?
- How can we enhance team knowledge?
- How do we motivate and encourage each other to have a positive culture?
- How can members and leaders coach each other to excel?
- How will members provide real-time feedback and hold each other accountable to achieve shared goals?
- How do members make suggestions for achievement celebrations or improvements?
- How do we go about bringing concerns, questions, and unresolved issues to the table? What can we do about them?
- How do we get agreement on public appreciation for work well done and giving improvement feedback privately?

Business performance (Goal setting, action plan, goal implementation, goal evaluation, and team efficiency)

- What would the goal setting and action plan implementation involve?
- How will we track the milestones?

- How will we assess the business/personal performance to date and determine the gap between targeted and actual activities?
- What worked well and what could be improved?
- Based on the lessons learned, what best practices could we develop for better performance and higher productivity?
- How will we translate the lessons learned to best practices or things to avoid?
- What tools will we use for problem-solving to build a productive team?
- How do we create a sound and timely decision-making processes where we consider everyone's viewpoint?
- What tools will we use to map the implementation process so that members know where the handoffs are?

Set the success principles jointly with all the team members in the early phases so that people are clear about team expectations, standards, goals, and implementation. It also provides members a chance to air any concerns before execution.

Implementation

The members and the leaders trust each other to do their jobs while holding each other accountable. Members step into a leader's role when the situation demands or when they take it upon themselves to improve the process.

First and foremost, the leader sets the example. If the leader is confident and upbeat, the team will feed off this. Likewise, if the leader is constantly down in the dumps, the team will feel as if a black cloud is hovering over them.

Leaders and members consistently communicate with each other to:

- Ensure the goals are on track.
- Proactively address potential challenges and problems.
- Continuously make an effort to build and sustain a collaborative environment where every member's strengths are leveraged appropriately and appreciated.

You achieve big things with small beginnings. There is no right time to create a strong collaborative and cohesive team. Every team member should work on it all of the time. Take action at every opportunity to develop a cohesive team.

Dedicated Teambuilding Time and Events

At regular intervals or specially coordinated events, designate time for the members and leaders to connect with everyone. Set aside time to air out concerns and frustrations while encouraging and empowering them with support and tools to become confident, independent, and interdependent.

A good idea is inviting members to plan the teambuilding activities.

Summation – Impact to Business

Cohesive teams with a common goal and purpose make sound decisions and achieve goals. You can have a room full of people with MBA's, Ph.D.'s, and leaders in their fields, but if you cannot get them to work well together, you are not going to advance your business the way you want. While it is a challenge to bring diverse people together with different personalities and backgrounds, when you are able to achieve it, you can move mountains.

There is a simple assignment done in many leadership courses showing the value of a team. The room is broken up into groups of six to eight people. The instructor tells everyone that they crashed on a desert island, and gives everyone a list of 15 or so items that were salvaged. As an individual, you have to assign a priority to each of the items with "1" being the highest until you rate all of them. Then as a group, you do the same thing. 95% of the time, the group result more closely matches the correct order of things as established by the US Army's survivalist experts.

The results are phenomenal when you have a bunch of people thrown together for a one-time task. Just imagine how you can increase and develop the synergy of your team that you build who come together to work. It takes mindfulness to accomplish a successful relationship with team as it does with all the relationships.

Having a relationship with team means that you have to check your ego at the door. There is a saying that if you are the smartest person in the room…then you are probably not hiring the right people! The genuine value of a team is where everybody who is a part of the team, even the leader, can learn from others. When this happens, then you know the team is a cohesive group functioning the way it should.

Build relationships among the team on the value of humanity and on the foundation of caring for others' well-being, such that your interaction makes your ideal clients feel important and an integral part of your life. Engage employees as equal contributors, leaders, and partners in business. Your clients will come to appreciate how your company performs and will seek you out for future business. People like to work with a business they perceive has its act together.

Probably the most critical assignment a leader has when developing a team is that of bringing out the best in them. As the saying goes, "Mighty oaks from little acorns grow." When a good leader sees the potential in an employee, he or she will be able to unlock that person's potential. All of the factors lead to a company's success.

You can have all the metrics in the world to chart your company's performance. Don't get me wrong; they serve a purpose. However, if you do not know how to maximize the talents and potential of everyone on your team, those metrics will never rise to where you want them. For an entrepreneur, the relationship with team is everything. Take the time to learn the skills you need to turn this relationship into an art form. You will never look back.

Exercise from a Team Member's Perspective:

These questions are designed to obtain real-time feedback from team members. The questions focus on what is important to the team members.

- Am I clear on my expectations with regards to my role and responsibilities in the team?
- Am I clear on the vision, mission, and values of the organization?
- Are my vision, mission, and values aligned with that of the organization?

- Do I have all the resources I need to do my job beyond expectations?
- Are my strengths being leveraged in the right area?
- Am I being appreciated on a regular basis?
- Are there opportunities for my personal development, learning, and growth?
- Do other team members care for, respect and support each other?
- Are my opinions regularly sought out?
- Am I aware of my career trajectory?
- Do I have conversations to measure work progress?
- Do I trust all team members?
- Am I willing to participate in open discussions and express my opinions without the fear of repercussions?
- Do I think that differences of opinion and perspective are valued?
- Are my contributions to the team appreciated?
- Do I train cross functionally, step into different roles, and perform various functions as needed?
- Do I make effective decisions to ensure excellent quality of products or services while maintaining high productivity?
- Am I committed to the team's success?

CHAPTER 8

PURPOSEFUL PARTNERS

A friendship founded on business is a good deal better than a business founded on friendship.

John D. Rockefeller

It was another beautiful day on the beach. As we walked, I finished recapping with Dee how I had strengthened my relationship with my team. "Taking action on what you have taught me has proven that these relationship principles work in real life. I have hired a third person for my firm. I created a talent profile and used that to guide me to hire the right person. I definitely hit a home run with this one. She stepped into the role so effortlessly that it feels as though we have been working together for years."

Dee clapped her hands. "That's so good to hear, Sally. What other principles have you implemented?"

After reflecting for a moment, I answered. "I invested part of the profits in a few operating systems to help my employees do their best. Most importantly, personal coaching has unleashed the potential of the one employee that I was having issues with in regards to his performance. I now trust him, and his enthusiastic attitude is contagious."

"Your company is moving forward in the right direction," said Dee.

"It has grown to the place that I envisioned when I first decided to go into business," I told her. I reached out and gave Dee an affectionate hug. "I needed the right mentor to set me on the correct path."

She returned the hug. "You know, Sally, I experience the same joy and gratification that you feel with your employees when I see you realizing your potential. I had a gut instinct about what you could do. That's why I wanted to work with you. Has your role changed in your business with the various successes you have accomplished?"

"Finally, I am not worried about, or working on, every facet of my business. I feel like a real CEO, and I like it. It feels like it is time to expand my business. You've given me the tools I needed to get to this point."

"What ways are you looking to expand?" asked Dee.

"I have been thinking of something you mentioned when we were talking about the relationship with team. It has to do with starting to seek out partnerships that will open up more opportunities for me."

Dee slowly nodded. "You remember me saying that! Well, relationship with partner is the next logical chain of progression as you get your business running the way you desire. It is a natural step to begin exploring growth opportunities. To start you thinking in the direction of finding the *right* partnership, let me share few questions with you." She smiled. "I know you, and you are going to want to write these down."

We sat on the sand, and I took out my trusty notebook. I came to think of it as the "Wisdom of Relationships." I wrote down the questions she gave me:

1. Do I want to remain a solopreneur or add on a partner?

2. What are my business goals? Do my business goals include a partner?

3. What kind of partnership fits my business goals?

4. What is the potential partner going to bring to the table and what is it that I need from a potential partner?

5. What is your potential partner's financial situation? Are they willing to invest what is necessary?

6. What are the potential partner's expectations of time involvement?

7. Is your potential partner committed to your business success as you are?

8. What is the business priority in your potential partner's life?

9. Is your potential partner capable of handling the droughts and downpours of the business season?

10. Is your potential partner credible and willing to sign a contract to pre-empt any future conflicts and create an exit plan if the partnership does not work out?

11. What values are important to your potential partner? Are your values aligned with those of that person?

12. What are the most important goals you want to achieve within the duration of your partnership?

Feeling perplexed, I looked up at Dee, invoking her laughter. She said, "I know. You are thinking, 'Why is everything more complicated than you initially thought?'"

"Yes, but I am aware that these complex questions have a purpose so that an entrepreneur, like me, is forced to think through the entire process. In which case, he or she…or me in this case…is able to make good choices right out of the gate," I replied proudly with a light-hearted laugh. "As someone who has benefitted from your lessons, I appreciate your method. I am living proof that it works."

"Yes, you are. Entering partnerships invites the same mindfulness as other relationships we have discussed. How far are you into exploring partnerships?"

"I've been thinking about partnerships a great deal, but have not acted on it yet," I said. "I'm not sure what direction I want to go in."

Dee replied, "Let's look at this from a different perspective. We'll do an exercise. Write down the people, other than your team members, who help you in the operations of your business."

I thought about this and pulled up a clean page in my notebook. I started writing and kept at it for five minutes. There were more people than I expected. I had a bookkeeper, CPA, lawyer, insurance broker, financial planner, virtual assistant (VA), web designer, graphic designer, and an information technology person who helped me with the back end systems for my business. There was also a photographer, videographer, editor, and Dee herself. When I finished reading my list, I looked up at Dee and she smiled.

"You see, Sally, you are already involved in some informal types of partnerships to keep your business thriving. We don't always think of relations with those professionals that help us with pieces of our company as partners, but they are. Relationship with partners is similar to a vegetable garden. You can scatter various kinds of seeds and have carrots growing with the tomatoes or the lettuce with the eggplant, but that makes it harder to give each vegetable the particular care they need. Each plant is unique. So, you group them by type. Partnerships are the same. You have those who help with the running of your business and those that actively help you grow your business. Then you might have those partnerships where you are working with them to help their organization or nonprofit. The lessons are the same for having a relationship with partners, but different associations have their unique qualities you have to be aware of." She paused for a minute and looked at my list again. "How is it working with them?"

"Except for a few, I have great relationships with these partners."

"Always be mindful of strengthening your healthy relationships. Then you need to evaluate the ones that are not so good and see what changes can be implemented to enhance them."

"This is a different relationship than I have with my team?" I asked.

"Yes, what I am talking about here is your relationship with those you do not directly employ or contract. Although partners are often not involved in the day-to-day running of your business, they are deeply involved in the strategy and execution, collaboratively within their area of expertise.

"So how does this relationship with partners work?"

"Help me up off the sand, Sally. We'll go back to my house and I'll make lunch. We can talk about it there."

"Do you like to cook?" I asked her as I helped her to her feet.

"Used to hate it. Never had time. However, when I had my companies perking along where I didn't need to be around every second, I went to Paris and became a Cordon Bleu Chef. Now, I love it."

We went back to her home, had a fabulous lunch that would rival any I ever ate, and talked into the night. Here is what I learned about having a relationship with partners.

What is Relationship with Partners

Business is a system in which all parts and processes contribute to the success or failure of the whole. Business partners come in different forms. You might want partners who share in every aspect of your company from the initial establishment to turning it into a sustaining success. The purpose may be to partner up for one particular project. Generally, the partner would be someone who specializes in a different industry than yours, but his or her company complements yours perfectly because the partner brings a different perspective to business operations. By joining forces, you grow together.

Whatever your intention is with a partner, it is important to realize that it is about collaborating, not competing. You are pooling resources of the mind and heart. With your partner, you want to create more opportunities, create more emotional and financial wealth, and go beyond what you can do alone.

Your growing business needs the support of an interdependent community of business partners, for example, VA, book co-writer, editor, copywriter, graphic designer, photographer/videographer, Joint Venture (JV) partners, chartered accountant, lawyer, etc. The primary goal of the relationship is that it is mutually beneficial for each side. If it is one-sided, it is not a partnership.

It is important to know that partnerships are defined in two major categories: Formal and Informal. Even the simplest of partnerships requires the agreement of a shared goal or set of solutions for the work to be performed. For example, your partnership with your CPA falls in the simple, informal category. It requires you to have a shared goal of being responsible for tax issues. Your CPA would be expected to provide you with updated solutions addressing the current tax year, and any past years tax concerns. An informal partnership may include barter or some other means of trade. It is a relationship based upon an interest or need that benefits two or more parties. It might include a contract defining the work and compensation, but it does not include a legal contract clarifying the goals, roles, and responsibilities of each party.

A formal partnership, on the other hand, is one where the partners share in the profits and liability of a venture. You formalize it by the signing of a contract that documents all aspects of the agreement, including the roles of both partners. Formal business partnerships must be mutually beneficial and thoroughly thought out.

Why Every Aspect of the Partnership is Important to

Business

When Dee emphasized that the relationship had to be mutually beneficial and thought out, I wasn't sure what she meant. Dee shared a story about one of her clients, Diane. Diane and her close friend had an excellent idea about a pet spa and decided to start the business together. They were excited about the new venture. They agreed to share in decision-making while splitting the workload and revenue equally. Because each knew several pet owners, their business took off. They brought in clients and began living the life they wanted.

After a year, Diane's friend started working on a new project. It took so much of her time that she began lagging in making decisions and was putting in fewer hours than Diane by a large margin. This frustrated Diane to no end and she was verging on exhaustion doing everything herself. As a result, the quality of the work suffered and clients became dissatisfied.

One day, when a client was complaining, Diane's partner came into the store. The partner said Diane was not pulling her weight. That was the last straw for Diane and she yelled back what had been on her mind for several months. Diane's friend calmed down and became quiet all of a sudden. Then she said, "Sorry, Diane. I think it is time we split up because I love my new business and do not have the time to spend at the spa."

Unfortunately, their legal contract did not capture how to resolve disputes and how to handle a buyout. Diane had to buy out her partner's side of the business, which was a drawn-out, expensive, and emotionally draining process.

The lesson of the story was that a formal business partnership is doomed to fail without the proper planning and consideration. Dee further clarified this concept to me by sharing Investopedia's definition of a formal partnership:

A partnership is an arrangement in which two or more individuals share the profits and liabilities of a business venture. Various arrangements are possible: all partners might share liabilities and profits equally, or some partners may have limited liability. Not every partner is necessarily involved in the management and day-to-day operations of the venture. In some jurisdictions, partnerships enjoy favorable tax treatment relative to corporations[5]

When entering into a formal business partnership, work out the details with a good lawyer experienced in the subject. You will need an agreement that describes methods for making business decisions, resolving disputes, consideration if one partner wishes to leave, and even what happens when a partner dies.

For the remaining part of this chapter, I am not addressing the formal type of partnership where two business owners come together to start a business. What I am describing here, and what Dee focused on, are those partnerships that do not require extensive legal setup. Based on our talks and experience, the partnerships Dee and I discussed are:

Business Systems Operations Partnerships

Whether you have a business or an organization, these system operation partners keep your business operating smoothly. These business partners may include at a minimum: virtual assistant, book co-writer, editor, copywriter, graphic designer, photographer, videographer, mentor/coach, sponsors, advocates, Joint Venture partners, strategic alliances, chartered accountant, and lawyer.

Joint Ventures (JV)

JV is a business endeavor undertaken by two individuals, businesses, or organization to share expenses or profits to achieve specific objectives. The commitment between the two parties might be through trust or a simple legal contract. The duration of a joint venture can be from a few months to several years. The parties may form a new identity or create a new co-brand.

---

[5] http://www.investopedia.com/terms/p/partnership.asp#ixzz4IdFQZy61

Strategic Alliances

This is an agreement for collaboration among two individuals, businesses, or organizations to achieve shared objectives.

Mentor/Mentee

This relationship is the top of the scale regarding business partnerships. A mentor is someone you can go to for advice, guidance, and honest evaluations. The relationship I have with Dee is a great example. As you have seen in the course of this book, she has been my mentor. She knows a lot more about being an entrepreneur than me as benefitted her experience and success. She unselfishly shared everything in this book with me.

Coach/Coachee

Here, two individuals are committed to working together to determine goals, create an action plan, and implement that action plan to accomplish the goals in this partnership. The coach's skills, experience, and adaptability serve as the nutrients for the client's success. During the process, confidence, trust, and mutual reliance bloom and act as a weed killer for doubts, negativity, and failures.

Champions

These people resonate with your purpose and vision. They recognize that your products and services are unique and promote them to others. Champions may or may not be your clients.

You may utilize any combination of these partners in your business. In general, partnerships allow you to:

- Reach a wider market with complementary products and services, increase sales, and magnify business growth.

- Co-brand products and services.
- Leverage additional talents/skills to jointly develop and sell a solution unique to the target market and achieve greater fulfillment and financial results.
- Share business risks, expenses, and save money, time, resources, responsibilities, and energy.
- Pooling of expertise, talents, energy, time and resources for large projects.
- Mutually support and motivate each other.
- Add value to widen your perspective on strategies to grow the business.
- Benefits the participating parties and their teams, customers, and clients.

How to Strengthen Your Relationship with Your Partners

Based on the Interlude chapter that covered networking, you have been connecting with your contacts, learning about people, helping them to excel, and gaining valuable insights and vital lessons for future relationships. As you build your relationships, you make an effort to bond in casual and fun ways and get to know more about people's interests, dreams, vision, hopes, and family. From that information, you can figure out how you can help them. Continue using the Interlude chapter's principles for cultivating potential partners.

Assuming you know which partnerships work best for you, seek out the right partner. The potential partner might already belong to your network. A solid relationship forms the foundation of a stable partnership. Continue building upon it. Once you have the right systems, right processes, and right people, it is possible to build long-lasting and resilient partnerships that are adaptive to a changing environment and deliver in the face of pressure.

Processes and Systems

As we said in the last chapter, a process is a series of structured events or activities to help you complete a task, project, or goal whereas a system is the "what" that is used to implement the process. For example, you need an affiliate platform for partnership so that you create the reports that show joint sales and can pay out the profits to your joint venture partner.

It is crucial to invest in systems with capabilities of scalability so that when your business grows, you do not need to spend and relearn new systems. Your business needs to be automated to run smoothly and allow you to do what you do best.

When the processes and systems are involved, then you might find that you are not ready for partnering because they are too laborious to accommodate changes that a partnership would bring. On the other hand, efficient systems allow you to improve and simplify the process. When the business systems and processes as a whole are simplified, you observe that you are able to handle the partnerships smoothly. You will have happy partners who are amenable to co-creating bigger opportunities because you prepared for such growth ahead of time.

Determining the Right Partner

It takes energy and time to build a relationship. It is important to match yourself with the right partner that has the correct values and skills. At any given time, when the intensity of a joint product or service launch is high, partners may have different priorities resulting in a mediocre or failed joint endeavor. In such a case, you or your partners might not want to continue with the next project. The discord results in lost trust and lost opportunities. Any momentum you have gained together, you have lost.

When you approach every partner discussion with the mindset of how you can help them, your return will be exponential. Because they know you from your network or a trusted friend introduces both of you, you can have a conversation to explore mutually beneficial opportunities.

When you evaluate potential partners that provide services like social media management, website design, etc., it is important to see the work they have done for others. Evaluating service providers include observing what others are saying about their work ethics, if you get along well with them, and if they will be able to understand your business values and purpose. For example, if a social media manager knows your ideal client, they will post relevant material that appeal to that potential client. This knowledge builds trust between you and that ideal client. If they are not the right fit and do not understand you, they could be posting material that does not speak of your values or does not target the best prospective clients. In such a case, you would have to monitor what they are posting, taking precious time away from you.

Similar to selecting ideal team members, you can use the same criteria in getting a feel about your prospective partner. Use behavior based questions to determine the values of the possible partner as well as their work ethic and passions. Listen to their answers. Over time, you can establish the profile of the type of partner that works well with you.

Look for a partner that has a similar purpose/vision. A business partner's vision tells you about a business' entire strategy and is fundamental to a company's future success. Purpose motivates each partner's actions and makes him or her more productive. Your co-brand, products, or services that you sell together should reflect your purpose. For example, part of your profits supports a cause so that your venture makes both societal and commercial sense.

Seek a partner whose motivation and drive match that of yours. You should both be willing to put in the same amount of time, resources, and energy to make your venture a success. You need to match each other in passion and motivation. Be open in communication with each other and continuously build on each other's trust.

It is also important to respect the contributions of your partner's team, and you should work at upholding each other's reputation. One partner doesn't carry another. It is a real partnership.

Bringing out the Best

The focus is one of a real relationship filled with appreciation and acknowledgment for each other. Together, you want to bring value and benefits to your partners and customers. Committed collaborators help each other be more, do more, and achieve more by focusing on their strengths while managing their shortcomings. It is about being realistically positive, instilling confidence in each other, and celebrating every win.

When collaborators know that customers may redefine the venture, the unexpected may require them to adjust the course. Partners look at the challenges as opportunities to learn, grow, and share the risk. Trust, transparency, flexibility, agility, and adaptability become an essential ingredient for the growth of business where collaborators are committed to each other. Customer satisfaction and their mutual success supersede personal success. Mutually attuned partners are able to bring out the best in each other as individuals as well as galvanize others on a joint business team with enthusiasm.

Be sure to partner with collaborators who are willing to step into a leader's role from the beginning. The best partners accept responsibility and provide a right balance of skills, abilities, and career aspirations. Determine the responsibilities of each collaborator for successful action plan implementation and project completion.

Regardless of who your collaborator is the following guiding principles can support you in building stronger, focused, and cohesive partnerships.

Commitment to Collaboration

Both parties have a substantial commitment to the collaboration. Work on a small project as an experimentation to iron out any wrinkles before the launch of a massive project. Ensure that there is a compelling reason for coming together such as a shared purpose, collective goals, or the desire to work together with like-minded powerhouses.

Various Phases of Partnership

Partnerships go through different phases of development. In the initial phase, you move from contact to a connection to collaboration. You become familiar with each other's personalities, purpose, vision, values, and goals. Then you have conversations to discover what works best for both parties and set up a simple legal contract that satisfies both. You set mutually beneficial goals for the new business endeavor, plan how to achieve the goals, implement the action plan, jointly evaluate the process, performance, wins, and gaps (Action Exercise at the end of this chapter: Purposeful Partnership Pulse Check provides a baseline). You do this at regular time intervals and adapt accordingly.

Setting Goals

Partners set mutually agreed clear goals using SMART (simple, measurable, achievable, relevant, and trackable) metrics for both the process and desired outcomes. Specific goals allow everyone involved to focus. Communication between partners promotes clarity about the goals and knowledge about how to guide everyone's efforts for goal achievement.

Everyone needs to be aware that they have a voice in determining how the partnership will work and that they are able to impact the emotional and financial outcomes. Partners need to know the consequences or failures that an organization will face from a dissonant partner that does not perform well.

Alignment of personal and organizational vision, mission, and values give a sense of direction, clarity, and drive for productivity:

- Both parties come together and mind map what the relationship between the two partners will be.
- Brainstorm together the values that are essential for the relationship to thrive.
- After brainstorming, individually evaluate each value on a scale of one (least important) to five (most important).
- Review the results together and talk about the values that are significantly different for each partner.
- Evaluate the gap between where your relationship is and where you want it to be. Determine what needs to be done to bridge the gap.

Institute your partner-specific "success principles" for planning execution

Successful partners usually exhibit a high level of personal respect shared by every member. They promote an environment of trust, candor, and open communication in which each person can contribute, question, and express their concerns. Partners understand that great relationships begin with an understanding of diversity.

Success principles are action-guiding principles that direct how interactions, work, and communication occur. As a leader, you open the floor for your partners to jointly create and agree upon an action plan.

Crafting the Success Principles and Action Plan:

- Agree on everyone's exact duties and responsibilities
- Balance the work equally between partners. In the same manner, have an agreement on splitting costs/profits, how the decision-making process works, etc. The more you can set down in writing at the beginning, the fewer issues you will face later.
- Be specific on what your mission is towards customers/clients.
- Have an exit strategy for any partner who wants to back out in the future: Determine timing, financial arrangements, etc.
- Set up success measurement checkpoints on how to chart the progress of your venture.
- Determine acceptable means of communication between partners.
- Establish manner of accountability.
- Figure out how to celebrate successes!

Success principles also set the stage for partners to air any concerns before execution. Everybody is in agreement and clear about expectations, standards, goals, and implementation when you set the success principles jointly with partners early in the game.

Implementation

Partners trust each other to do their jobs while holding each other accountable. They step into a leader's role when the situation demands or when they take it upon themselves to improve the process. As with any endeavor, the example of leadership within a partnership sets the tone. A positive outlook affects everyone; so do negative ones. Leaders need to:

Ensure the goals are on track.
- Proactively address potential challenges and problems.

- Continuously make an effort to build and sustain a collaborative environment where every member's strengths are leveraged appropriately and appreciated.
- Review the purposeful partnership pulse check (at the end of the chapter) to pinpoint exactly where the problem might be happening and resolving it before it escalates into an obstacle.

Small beginnings lead to significant results. There is no right time to create a strong collaborative and cohesive relationship among partners. Every partner should work on it consistently. Use every opportunity to grow and strengthen the bonds.

Dedicated Partner-building Time and Events

At regular intervals or specially coordinated events, designate time for the members and leaders to connect with everyone. During this period, everyone should feel free to air out concerns and frustrations. Also, encourage and empower members with support and tools to become confident, independent, and interdependent.

One other thing, don't be afraid to have fun when you are doing it!

Summation – Impact to Business

Seeking out and nurturing strong partnerships allows you many opportunities. It can grow your business or organization faster, enable you to start a different one, devote some time to a worthwhile cause dear to your heart, etc. Success can be exponentially increased whenever we collaborate with people with similar values and vision.

Nobody is good at everything. A good partner will be your strength in areas where you are weak, and you do the same for him or her. Together you have fun, learn from each other, and your reciprocal lessons will cultivate the venture you are doing together.

Challenges will show up along the way. These become catalysts for deep thinking and an opportunity to connect with values, requiring high levels of engagement to manage uncertainty and complexity. The sharing of risk allows partners to embrace experimentation, which leads to elevated levels of internal motivation that is contagious to other partners. People shift from ME performance to WE performance (ME when flipped is WE) moving towards mutual investment, participation, and holding each other accountable. Unsurprisingly, this type of relationship encourages trust and freedom to all members.

The cliché is that a relationship is 50-50. This is a misconception. For a successful relationship...and that is what a partnership is...to work, each member needs to bring 100% to the table. When every partner does that, you are going to open windows to financial success, personal fulfillment, and customer satisfaction that it is difficult to achieve alone. You will often find that a partnership will bring you into contact with more people who align with your vision and values than if you were by yourself. These are the potential partners for other endeavors.

Do not limit yourself to you. Seek out others where partnering is mutually beneficial and establish a plan to work together. You will find yourself surpassing your expectations of what you can achieve.

Purposeful Partnership Pulse Check Action Exercise

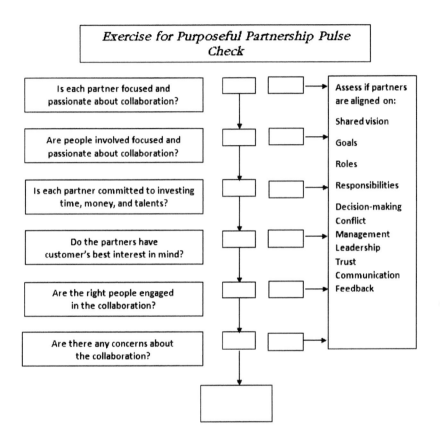

CHAPTER 9

THE DEATH OF FEAR

Meet life.
Change is constant.
Resist you can, escape you can't.
Death and Life, live together
Becoming one, forever
Life or Death
Choice is yours
Although fear is rife
Say, "Yes" to Life.

Divya Parekh

"You look very tan," said Dee as a way of greeting.

I was following her through her house out to the porch. A cold rain was falling, and I saw two steaming mugs of tea waiting for us on the coffee table in front of a couple of chairs.

Pleased with myself, I shared, "My two girlfriends and I went to Hawaii for two weeks. It is something that none of us thought possible a year ago. All three of us have benefited from your lessons, which I shared with them after applying them in my own business. They were pretty much in the same place I was twelve months ago, and are now about two months behind me on the success curve since I worked on each relationship before engaging them in the practice. We are all doing so much better. Not only was paying for the trip not an issue for me, but it was also a total vacation because I didn't have to worry about my business. I know my team is good at running things."

With a smile, Dee said, "I like how you refer to your employees as 'my team.' It is gratifying to me that you are sharing our talks almost as soon as you learn something new."

It was my turn to grin. "I think one of your conditions was to share all of this relationship expertise with others."

"And that unselfishness will take you far!" exclaimed Dee. "Besides bringing the balance of life with a nice vacation and having a solid team behind you now, what else have you been accomplishing?"

"I have been using the heart-mind share in my networking. I am always mindful of prioritizing my time. One of my biggest gains has come by expanding my business with partners. I have been cultivating an entrepreneurial culture that encourages team members and partners to promote and support each other."

Dee saw the small frown pass across my brow and quickly said, "But…"

I sighed. "Sometimes I am afraid that it will all disappear. Sometimes, I pinch myself to verify it is real. You know where my company was last year, and now it has expanded three-fold."

Dee asked, "Do you have enough money to survive during the rainy days?"

"Yes," I told her. "I set up my finances so that my contingency fund holds enough money to sustain the business and my lifestyle for at least a year, if need be."

"That's great!" Dee exclaimed. "It is a good safety net to have. Perhaps what we cover today will alleviate your concerns about your business success disappearing. I'm going to share a few thought-provoking questions with you. You might not think about them in your busy life, but they will most likely resonate with you."

I gave her a playful eye roll. "Always questions!"

"As I think you realize by now, young lady," she said with her grin, "that asking the right questions is the way to begin thinking in the correct direction on a subject."

She then handed me a paper with the following questions printed out:

1. If you were to start over again, would you do the same business or is there anything else you would rather be doing?

2. Do you refrain from investing in new opportunities because of the uncertainty of the outcome?

3. If you were to review your last year, how many remarkable moments can you recall?

4. Can you see past your fears and see the value of becoming more, doing more, and achieving more?

5. How close to death are you – to your death, to a loved one's death, to the possible end of your business?

6. Are your businesses and loved ones protected if anything happened to you?

I looked over the questions again. "Wow, this is profound stuff," I said. "Let me think a minute." I drank some tea and watched the rain fall outside. "I would get out of the corporate world and form my company again if I had to do it over." Looking at Dee, I added, "Of course, this time, I would start out with all of the knowledge you shared and skip the months of frustration."

Dee laughed aloud at that. "Smart girl. How about the rest?"

"I have a fear of sustaining my business over the long-term. Especially now that the business is performing as I originally dreamed."

"That fear is comparable to manure. It smells awful, but it fuels the growth," Dee assured

"I have to admit I haven't given a great deal of thought to everything else. I feel I have been sprinting for a long time now. Hawaii was the first time I felt I was able to catch my breath."

"Vacations are important, Sally. So is setting time aside for self-reflection and evaluation. As with everything else, you need to approach a relationship with death with the same mindfulness of everything else.

"Relationship with death!" I exclaimed, cocking my head in surprise.

What is Relationship with Death

"As they say, Sally, nothing is certain except death and taxes. Our society in the 21st century tries to insulate us from death. However, whenever we are close to it, it forces us to explore our thoughts and feelings about the subject. By doing so, it provides us the opportunity to live our life in a new and fulfilling manner."

"Am I supposed to approach this relationship with the same mindset as the others?" I asked.

"Definitely," responded Dee. "By doing so, you come to terms with the fact that fear is a part of life. This relationship is about accepting fear, working through it, and using the grit that you have deep inside of you to overcome it. It is about living life rather than passing through it. Shakespeare said, 'A coward dies a thousand times before his death, but the valiant taste of death but once.' By establishing your relationship with death, you learn to live with that fear in your life. It will help you overcome challenges, go after new opportunities, and set your affairs to take care of your loved ones and your business in the event of your death."

"Isn't that kind of a morbid thought?" I asked.

"On the contrary, it is freeing. I just turned 85, and I have had my plans in place for 50 years now. I update them periodically, but that is a fear I do not have anymore. Besides," Dee said with a twinkle in her eye, "I have another good 30 years in me. You see, when you are comfortable with the fact that you will die someday or that something happens where you can't run your business, you will have created a sustainability plan that will support your team, your family, and your clients.

Why Relationship with Death is Important to Business

It was at this point that Dee started to tell me about her relationship with death and how it evolved for her. I took out my smartphone and began recording it:

You know, Sally, we take great pains to insulate ourselves from death. We see death on the news all the time, but unless it is someone close to us, we have an almost "it is not real" attitude towards it. We know it happened, but we can keep it at arm's length.

Now, when we have a close brush with death, whether our own or a loved one, our perspective about life changes 180 degrees. It is sad that we have to get that close to death or something terrible to look at life with new eyes. Why wait until that happens? Why not take stock of where we are right now and yell out "yes" to life without the traumatic experience? It saves a lot of energy, time and grief!

When we do that, we not only appreciate life more, but we want to live life to its fullest. When you are living your life, you see everything with new eyes…seeing new possibilities where we saw none before. You find yourself gaining happiness with mindfulness, grace, and gratitude. You understand that staying true to yourself brings peace as nothing else does.

As you reach this magical place in life, you find that you can take yourself and your business beyond the expected by being more, doing more, and achieving more. Life and business becomes a playground where you enjoy the fruits of your play.

Years ago, I heard a TED Talk titled "The Golden Circle" by Simon Sinek. It introduced a defining moment in my life. If you haven't seen it, you should check it out on the Internet. As I watched it several times, I explored my current business while focusing on the original "Why" I was in business. For me, it was always about my love of people and having a connection with others.

A few months after the insight of my Why, I broke my right arm in multiple places near the shoulder, and the joint became calcified. I have to say that this injury humbled me to a level that I never imagined. I did not realize that I was taking "Everyday Life" for granted.

After the injury and resulting complications, I often crowned myself "The Poor Me Grumpy Queen." My world had diminished to a small area of existence, with only a few resources within my reach. Since my ability to move without excruciating pain was so profound, I set up a recliner in my living room. I sat there by day, and slept (or tried to) by night. I could no longer drive, write, type, prepare food, shower, change clothes, or get up from that darned chair without help. I was experiencing life as an invalid; something that I didn't think would happen until a very old age – if at all.

I yearned for the ability to do simple chores such as opening a car door, getting up unassisted, eating without dropping crumbs all over, sleeping on a bed instead of a recliner, and listening to music instead of the painful drumbeat of my arm.

I repeatedly crumbled under the weight of the crown and made efforts to rise, but only dissolved again in frustration. At times, when I was barely taking care of personal needs, I could not think about business. When I thought of my business that solely depended on me, a fog of fear would envelop me to the extent that I was not able to think clearly. I felt distressed because not only was I physically in pain, but I was also dealing with mental, emotional, and financial burdens to carry on my one good shoulder and one broken shoulder. I thought my business was going to shatter into little pieces like glass. I didn't think my business or I would ever be the same again. All was gloom and doom!

Then, one day, I was fortunate to fall into a deep meditation after taking pain medication. I realized I had enough. I made a split-second decision to create a shift. After that, although my emotions were swinging from low to high, I learned to live by the phrase "necessity is the mother of invention." During my reflective, positive waves, I began to garner my mind, emotions, and actions for the arduous journey of recovery. I often thought of my "Why", reminding myself that it's about my love of people and connections.

I began to allow myself to be vulnerable, to put my pride on the back burner, and ask for help. Surprisingly, the relationship bonds with my closest friends and colleagues became very robust. The more I asked for help, the more people offered. It was a very eye-opening concept that I began to explore in depth. I wondered what made these great people so willing to help me, even beyond what I asked.

I reached further into my shrunken circle of resources, asking how I could understand a never-explored depth of value from each of them. My friends, experiences, meditation and mindfulness and even that darned recliner became a pillar of exploration. Failed efforts did not matter as long as I got back on my feet again. Practicing gratefulness, I began to feel very fortunate that I had these incredible resources and their new offerings of support and hope. I learned the true difference between acceptance and giving up.

I was fortunate that people cared deeply for me. When people asked me how I broke my arm, I shared three stories for them to pick from: I was skydiving and fell on a herd of buffaloes; I got into a bar fight; or I landed on the boat while tubing on the lake. It taught me to shift the sympathy to humor and give back a moment of laughter to friends and family when I thought I did not have anything to give.

At first, I had a misconception that my injury stole a year out of my life. I later realized that it provided me with the equivalent of years of learning, growing, and gaining momentum in a relatively short period. I experienced a shift in perspective and actions where I was able to receive and give back. I supported my relationships by listening to their woes and challenges as well as helping them in their personal and professional growth.

I crossed the challenges, gained a deeper clarity about my vision, published books on Amazon, and developed my signature program of nine relationships that are the pillars of entrepreneurial success. I continued to interview people for my radio show and forged new and deeper partnerships. What I thought might be the death knell for my business became a wave of creativity and ingenuity that kept my business alive and thriving.

I was also able to keep somewhat of a routine personal and home life with the help of friends and family. I spent quality time with them and continued with my physical and mental self-care.

As the end of the year approached, I spent some time in reflection and I was pleasantly surprised that I kept my sanity through it all. I stayed true to my "Why." I had a massive personal evolution. I found that I continued to serve my relationships with new and ever more insightful offerings. I contributed to the evolution of our great planet through people like you, Sally, as well. Based on that experience, I also started putting things in place for my businesses to account for the eventuality of death. The contingencies make it necessary to accept the fears, engage with those fears through mindfulness, and to move beyond the fears. Freedom awaits you beyond the fears.

How to Strengthen Your Relationship with Death

Dee's story compelled me to think about these questions that I hadn't pondered until now. I would prefer to tap into that feeling towards life and my business without having to go through any painful and harrowing event in my life. I asked her how to work on my relationship with death and avoid waiting for some life-changing event to affect me. The rest of this chapter is her words of wisdom on the subject.

Whether you are starting a business, are a struggling entrepreneur or a success, you only have so many moments, months, and years. Obstacles and challenges come your way, but so do peace, joy, and love. As you learn and practice the relationships you have learned so far, you have been developing fortitude that makes you strive continuously towards your vision. Your "Why" is the vision that fuels you with unending reservoirs of enthusiasm, introspection, self-discipline, and the push to persevere towards the destination of success without worrying about encumbrances.

The fruit of peace and pride in your efforts coupled with the joy, evolution, and coherence of the process that you come to experience are the results of discipline and contemplation. You transcend beyond consciousness to experience timelessness. When this peace pervades your business through actions, there is no desperation, only action…only Karma. You extend this peace and pragmatism to the future of your business to secure the future of your loved ones, business, and community. You know that strife and setbacks still occur, but so does the discipline. You know you will continue to break those clouds and let the sun shine.

Scanning the Future

Thinking about death requires rising above the normal thinking and connecting with the realm of spirituality as defined by you. It is up to you how to define it. Spirituality is the anchor that helps you transform the fear to the independence of mind and spirit. Spiritual growth leads to enhanced mindfulness creating a harmony in all you do. When you face the fear of moving forward to your desired goals, follow this process:

1. Your vision, built on your "Why," is the driving force behind your planning and efforts. As things change, revisit your vision. Remember why your vision is important to you. Then your mission, values, and goals will come back into focus to ensure that your planning is relevant. The vision to become a hugely successful entrepreneur, have harmonious and loving relationships, educate people about entrepreneurial leadership, and leaving enough wealth for loved ones, charities, and other communities.

2. Based on your discovery from Step 1, reprioritize your goals in relation to their importance.

3. Identify your support systems. These are all the financial and emotional assets that will help you in the time of unexpected events like health or accident issues. They safeguard your loved ones and your business after your death. For example, it could include:

- Successful business (one or more)
- Strong financial plans, such as 401K and pension plans
- Lack of debt
- Self-discipline and investment habits

4. Identify existing or potential challenges that may prove to be hindrances in the path of vision achievement. For example:

- Family or business partner conflicts
- Accident or sickness
- Business failure
- A loved one's death
- Your death
- Hating your business or job
- Financial debt

Achieving Heart and Mind Harmony

When you think about death, debts, and seemingly insurmountable challenges, your fears and inertia will cause you to experience a wall of resistance. You think, "None of this will happen to me." It is important to remember that the "process" that you experience every step of the way on your journey fulfills your life. The moments of accomplishment are fleeting. It is like a beautiful flower blooming, and then the petals fall off.

It is helpful to know how the typical journey goes as you strive for the pinnacle to heart and mind harmony. To illustrate it better, think of it as this pyramid.

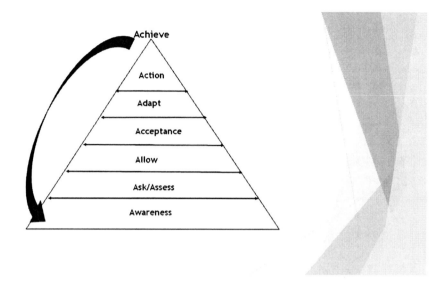

Success Pyramid

1. Awareness (First A of the Pyramid) Raise self-awareness by observing the connection between the fear or discomfort and your choice of action or inaction. If you are taking action, are you taking action toward your goals or actions that sabotage your success? If it is inaction, is it to reflect upon fear and develop the grit to move through the fears, or is it feeling sorry for yourself that brings you down?

2. Ask/Assess (Second A) the situation, your thoughts, your choices. Focus on what you can change. The step includes leaving the past where it belongs whether it is your thinking, your actions, your environment, etc.

3. Allow (Third A) yourself to pause and experience the moment.

4. Accept (Fourth A). Bring mindfulness to the choice you are making without judgment. As you turn inward, write down your top five fears, five things you are grateful for, your top five values, your top five strengths, and your top five achievements in the past week.

When you review the list, you will discover that you achieved goals during the week despite your fears.

5. Adapt (Fifth A) - If mindfulness is not on the menu, shift your attention to something else as in exercise, nature walks, breathing control, dancing away the energy of fear, or engaging in what you fear.

6. Action (Sixth A) Think about consequences before you make a choice and take action. If it is the right action, take it!

7. Achieve (Top of the Pyramid) - As you stay the course and focus on your goal from a place of peace, you will achieve success.

When you face fear, repeat the process again. You will still experience fear; the only difference is you know how to work through it.

Achieving Business Harmony

When you look at the business from a place of clarity and fearlessness, you will act wisely to grow your business, ensuring its success and sustainability. When you prepare for the eventuality of death, the right financial advisor guides you in the right direction. The following information does not replace seeking support from a financial advisor. At a minimum, you should research the following:

- Invest time to find a reputable certified financial planner advisor, who comes highly recommended from a trusted source, who matches your vision, mission, values and goals, and who will look out for you. This professional will understand you better, help you gain clarity to determine your support systems for your loved ones and business, and provide you with relevant and applicable solutions. When you implement these solutions, you are able to achieve your goals. Usually, your goals consist of:

- Replacing income, maintaining your lifestyle, and achieving future goals for you and your loved ones.
- Determining the fate of costly or unnecessary assets like vacation homes, extra vehicles, etc.
- Having funds for maintaining your business by loved ones or partners, or allowing for the buyout of the company by your partners. Pertinent estate taxes also need to be figured into the equation.
- Investments for supporting social and community projects.
- Emergency funds.

- Figure out THE FIGURE (your financial assets and your income potential for the rest of your working years). The FIGURE is the amount of money needed to secure your present lifestyle and business in case of unexpected events or death.
- Identify your financial stage. For example, if you are in the financial dependence stage where you need to close the gap between your current and future state, then the planning includes wills, trusts, life and business insurance for any risks of liability arising from business activity. During the years the business is in existence, you must take steps to minimize the possibility of liability resulting from the business activity.
- A personal life insurance policy can substitute your income and protect your loved ones by helping them cover regular expenses, college costs, or a mortgage balance. It is important to earmark your life insurance to support your business should you or one of the partners dies prematurely.
- Select the type of life insurance pertinent to your situation. Always consider your family first. Younger families look for income and maintaining a lifestyle whereas those who are older might use insurance as a mechanism to transfer wealth or a legacy to younger generations. Besides, as an entrepreneur, you need insurance for income replacement and protecting the fate of your organization. Your planner helps you assess the pros and cons of your policies as they relate to your financial plan and the needs of your business. They can also guide you toward a highly rated insurance company. It

is important to ensure that the company will be around decades from now for your loved ones.

- It is possible that you are in the financial independence stage where you have THE FIGURE. During this juncture, protecting your wealth and assets is a priority along with planning for unexpected eventualities.
- If you are in the financial advantage stage, you can plan for transferring funds to heirs or have estate plans or trusts for a social capital legacy or a family foundation.

Summation – Impact to Business

Death is almost a taboo subject. Unless it has affected an individual in some way, no one speaks of it in conversations. The word death evokes discomfort and fear.

Fear is a useful thing to have because it makes you pause and helps you turn inwards. It causes you to reflect, learn, grow, and evolve. If you were always happy, you would not appreciate the times when you are free of fear. As we talk about death and share our experiences about it, it brings to the forefront that longevity is not as significant as your quality of lifestyle, how intensely you live, and how regret-free you conduct your life. When you shift the focus to life, the present moment, and working through fear, the fear dies and you live each moment fresh and young. When you bring a fun, young, and renewed perspective on life and business, you attract more people and clients. Often that perspective is what is missing in the lives of adults who are preconditioned by society expectations and norms.

Although your emergency plans for an accident, health concerns, or death might be complex and require intensive planning, the key is to find a certified financial planner today. You never know when it is too late to start using one or more of the plans, so the earlier, the better. It is important to determine the fate of your business wealth and debts that will occur after your death.

There are books devoted to business disposition and estate planning. It is a complex subject depending on the size of your business, your wealth, and the state you live in (laws vary). Quite often, a team of an experienced financial planner and an estate attorney can steer you through these complex decisions.

As a business owner, the thing you don't want to do is leave your business, team, partners, and clients high and dry in case of your demise or incapacity to run the company. Planning for these eventualities might be the last thing you want to do. However, thinking it through and acting on it will give you a sense of accomplishment, peace, and relief that will allow you to live life the way you want.

Success Pyramid Exercise

Take the time to go through the Success Pyramid. Write down your thoughts, feeling, and actions (or potential actions) as you go through steps 1-7. Use that as a launching pad to create your plan for a sudden change of circumstances. Talk to loved ones and partners. Bring in the professional advisors to make your plan happen and then implement it.

CHAPTER 10

LIVE YOUR LEGACY

Life is happening as we speak. Why wait to leave your legacy when you can live your legacy.

Live your legacy and leave your legacy.

Divya Parekh

I came across an envelope with familiar handwriting when I was going through my mail. When I opened it, I pulled out a card, displaying a picture of a beautiful mountain scene with the sun peering out over one of the peaks. When I opened it, a folded piece of paper fell out. I set the paper aside as I read Dee's note on the card.

Sally,
It was very gratifying to read today that you opened a branch of your business in another state. It is amazing to watch you grow so much as an entrepreneur and as a person in the past year. I am proud of you.
I am not sure if you had a chance to celebrate this newest accomplishment, but I want to invite you out to dinner on Thursday evening if you are available. Oh yes, I have included a few things for you to ponder before we get together. We can chat about them then.
Love,
Dee

I thought this was very sweet of her, especially when I saw the restaurant where she wanted to meet. It was the best around and hard to get a reservation.

Then I smiled. Only Dee would send homework before dining at such an establishment.

I unfolded the paper and looked at the questions she sent:

1. Do you feel fulfilled in your life, or do you feel you could be more, do more, and achieve more?

2. Do you have any regrets? If yes, is there anything you can do about them?

3. Do your children and family members know about the values, vision, and stories that shaped your family? Are they excited to hear the stories about the family history?

4. Do your family members show enthusiasm when they remember vacations or holiday gatherings?

5. How do your family members, friends, connections, team, partners, and clients feel about you? What do they say about you? Do they look forward to seeing you?

6. What is your intent in every interaction that you have with people on a daily basis?

7. Do your family members, friends, connections, team, partners, and clients value you and will they do something for you without asking them?

8. How do you define your legacy that you are living right now and will leave after death?

I put the paper down and sighed. The woman asks tough questions!

A car dropped me off in front of the restaurant. I wore a dark violet dress and new shoes I bought for the occasion. I went up to the maître d' and told him I was looking for Dee. Smiling, he said, "It will be my pleasure to show you to her table. She arrived a few minutes ago."

His admiring tone made me ask, "You said Dee's table?"

"Oh, yes, we always keep a particular table open for the owner. We never know when Dee is going to drop in."

I gasped as he led me through the elegant dining room. Dee sat behind a small, unobtrusive table in a corner. As the maître d' held my chair, I sat and greeted Dee with, "You own this magnificent place?"

She gave a small shrug, but with a twinkle in her eye said, "After I had learned to be a chef, I had to do something with the knowledge."

"You aren't the chef too, are you?"

"No, but Diego my head chef lets me come in and get creative with him when I have time."

I shook my head in amazement. As a waiter brought over our wine, we looked through the menu. Dee didn't bring up any of the questions she sent me until our plates were cleared away and we looked over the dessert menu. To say the meal was fabulous would be an understatement. It was only then that Dee asked me what I thought about her questions.

I said, "As usual, you had me thinking of things I have not considered at this point in my life. Our entire last session had me thinking about death, as I never had before. I never discussed it much with my family or friends. I always pretended that any fears I had about the subject weren't there. I realize now, though, that those apprehensions we discussed as part of the relationship with death occur unexpectedly at stressful times."

Dee said, "Whether you make a difference in your life, a loved one's life, or someone else's, one bleeds into another. When you are confident in your passion, you work at it. I had a passion for making a difference. I wanted to reach out and genuinely help others. I found opportunities to do that every day whether it was something small or in a larger endeavor."

"Doing something along those lines every day is mind-boggling," I exclaimed.

"Always remember, Sally, that the power of small actions is immense. For example, a smile can make someone's day. Mother Teresa summed it up beautifully. She said, 'If you are kind, people may accuse you of ulterior motives. Be kind anyway.' You know, people often talk about leaving their legacy for their loved ones and causes they support. However, I believe we need to start living our legacy now; as well as what we leave behind after our death."

What is Relationship with Legacy

"I imagine this is another relationship," I said.

After beckoning the waiter over and telling him that there was a special dessert in the kitchen for us, Dee answered. "Yes, this is the relationship with legacy. Legacy is expanding your gifts in a way that neighbors, the community, and the world may benefit whether you live it now, or you leave it upon your exit from this world. It can be tangible or ethereal. It is a deeper level than just living. By that, I mean it is not only taking care of yourself and your loved ones, but also making sure that your actions leave them, your neighbors, community, environment, and the world in a better state. It is about making every interaction count. It is about having a positive impact on others while you are alive, and how people remember you when you are gone. It is your gift to people that will outlast several generations. That gift can be a smile, a kind act, leadership, a book, a podcast, articles, videos, philosophies, products, or services that leave their mark on people and get passed on across generations."

"That is an excellent concept to wrap my arms around," I remarked. "I understand it, but are you saying that it is something I need to focus on now like the other relationships?"

"Certainly, Sally, and I will explain the philosophy of this concept. After dessert, you can pull out your phone. If you like, you can tape our conversation so you can mull it over later."

True to her word, a special treat did come to the table. It was a type of cake made up of a sinful combination of chocolate. On top was written, "Congratulations, Sally." When we finished and ordered more tea, I took out my phone and recorded the rest of what Dee told me about the relationship with legacy.

Good or Bad, Everyone Leaves a Legacy

It is important to realize that legacies can be both positive and negative, and you have a choice in which type to live and leave for the future. In the negative context, world history shows us the legacies of poverty, conflicts between countries, and misuse of power. In personal lives, we see the legacies of many dysfunctional behaviors, including addictions, laziness, abuse, and family feuds. In business, we see the outcome of greed, corruption, poor planning, and management. Now that you are made aware that you have a choice in which type of legacy to leave – good or bad, we will focus on the legacies with a positive impact

Why is Relationship with Legacy Important to Business

Let me break this down and first look at entrepreneurs. They are a special breed of people who become inspired by obstacles and challenges despite the burden of risk and potential failure. They are fueled by the burning desire to impact others. For that reason, they take action to combine out-of-the-box thinking with grit to provide a new or unique solution, product, service, or process to make a positive impact to others.

Entrepreneurs are viewed as change agents as they bring solutions to their patrons' problems. As an entrepreneur, you are already in the business of making your clients' lives better. Why not take it steps further and expand your reach to influence more people positively. You may be thinking, "Why do I need to do that?"

The distinction between the forest and the trees highlights the gap that is present between your world as you see it and the entire world out there. Your perceptions, beliefs, values, actions, environments, and the era of time you live in limit your perceptual reality. However, as an entrepreneur, you move out of your environment and become connected with the world as a whole through learning, science, technology, and communication. You understand that our planet goes beyond an individual's lifetime because its history spans thousands of years. When you look at the grandiose scope of our planet's history, evolutions, and the history of humans, it transcends your limited perceptual reality.

You might be living in a city's downtown area where you have the conveniences of modern life at your fingertips. At the same time, there is someone in the world who is happy just to have running water. Thinking about the forest as a whole planet and the tree as those you help allows you to become aware of the vast difference in peoples' lifestyles. This awareness sways your focus away from your life, and you rise above the forest to see the universe in its entirety. You grasp the relevant feeling of the whole infinite setup, the evolution of humanity over eons of time, and your life as a tree. Most fascinating of all is the dynamics of interplay between you and the world where the equilibrium can shift either way to meet the demands of the situation. The world supported you to grow and come into your own. Support yourself, humankind, and the world as a token of gratitude now that your individuality has fostered.

You are probably speculating the impact of a living legacy. Your living legacy can make a difference in your life, and that of your loved ones, friends, clients, and community. The good that you do is absorbed, transferred, or integrated by people in your life now and after your death. When you contribute to a cause greater than yourself, the results are infinite. However, you have to give without fanfare. Aim at supporting others to become happy, successful, and lead a better lifestyle. You will not only be happier at a cellular and spiritual level, but you will also help improve peoples' lives.

How Can You Strengthen the Relationship with Legacy

Dee shared a story that when she was in the corporate world, the company teams would donate money for heart walks and participate in 5Ks for various causes. She felt that something was lacking. Even when contributing, Dee did not feel fulfilled. After reflecting on her values, she realized that interacting with people was important to her. She loved coaching people and enjoyed the feeling of awe when people's eyes lit up with the dawn of awareness. She needed to be authentic to be truly useful. For her, that meant working and interacting with people genuinely to make a difference. The point is that the beauty and joy of living your legacy lies in simplifying the interacting dynamics between you and the world.

When you catch the giving bug, you start asking questions such as, "What is the best way to support people in their success?" Like other relationships, it begins with a plan as to whom you want to impact and how you will make this happen.

Through your business contacts and personal relationships, each person you lead to transformation is affected. Furthermore, that transfiguration affects those individuals in their circle of influence. Think about how your extended reach…your ripple effect…can impact scores of people because of one interaction between you and another soul. Regardless of how you leave your legacy, the goal is to create a connected, supportive community that helps its members.

Legacy through Wealth

There is a misconception that monetary legacies are only limited to rich people who donate money to build a school extension or a hospital wing. Many people leave behind real estate, a trust for loved ones, or something for their favorite charity.

Although you may not be in position to leave behind lots of money, you could dedicate one scholarship for a deserving student. A philanthropic gift makes a huge impact on changing the lives of many, but that alone does not define an individual's legacy. When it comes to leaving monetary legacies, one of the simplest ways is to designate a specific amount from 25 dollars to several hundred dollars in your financial budget every year to support the causes close to your heart. You can create a legacy in a number of ways, and money is a small part of the whole spectrum of legacy gifts.

Legacy through Heart and Mind Share

As you set out, remember to involve both heart and mind. A mantra to know is that you can only do heart and mind share with what you have. First, figure out your values (Relationship with Self Chapter): what is important to you, what gives you joy, and whom you want to impact. Once you have figured out the plan, act on it.

Legacy in Daily Life and Business

In personal life, you want to guide the next generation on how to live a life of values, be a good human being, and build character. The character will allow them to do the right thing, even under stress. Your memories and values live in them while you are alive, and even after your death.

Every action for yourself and others counts. Whatever you are doing, if you commit to yourself to be happy, you will impact others. A small rock can cause a ripple effect across the pond. Studies prove this. Let's look at one study by James Fowler, a University of California, San Diego, political scientist and Harvard University medical sociologist Nicholas Christakis. They followed 4,700 people over a period of 20 years.

The study established that a happy person's friend has a 25% increased chance of experiencing happiness. They also observed that a friend of that friend experiences an approximately 10 percent chance of greater happiness whereas a friend of that friend has a 5.6 percent increased opportunity of experiencing happiness. You would think that your happiness is dependent on your choices, actions, and experiences. However, Nicholas A. Christakis mentioned that other people's choices, actions, and experiences impact your happiness. Happiness is infectious.

Previous studies have demonstrated that one person's emotions can act as a stimulus for another person's emotions. For example, a happy and smiling individual uplifts someone else's spirits. The new study supports that happiness is contagious across groups over a prolonged period[6].

On a daily basis, you can create the living legacy model through The 1/1/1 Leader Project (Action Exercise), or create a simple living legacy model that you can repeat day in and day out. The 1/1/1 Leader Project pledge gives you the motivation to commit to your top goal, smile at someone to make his or her day, and do one kind act per day. When you are kind, compassionate, loving, generous, and grateful to others, you will feel happy. On a personal note, when you feel comfortable and happy, your family and friends will be happy and kind to others, creating the ripple effect.

On a business level, your happy and positive interactions with your team, partners, potential client, and clients builds their confidence and makes them happy. This leads to their success and ultimately your success. Additionally, studies have concluded that human genes respond positively to the pursuit of pro-social purposes. A positive feedback loop between kindness and happiness occurs that inspires others. As we build a connected community, goodness will emerge from all directions. Productivity will increase all around leading to intellectual and economic development[7].

---

[6] http://legacy.wbur.org/2008/12/05/harvard-study-happiness-really-is-contagious

[7] http://genomebiology.com/2007/8/9/R189/abstractLoneliness, Happiness Affect Gene Expression, Health

Legacy through Dedicated Time and Talent

You can commit anything from one hour to as much time as you can spare for something dear to your heart. You probably could:

- Share a skill or expertise with others.
- Volunteer for a particular cause or in an organization of your choice.
- Spend time with the next generation by being a big brother or a big sister to children and teach them life lessons through your personal stories, teach them financial goals, or go fishing and play ball.
- Dedicate time on social media or writing blog posts to spread the message of social harmony.
- Support recycling, saving energy and water where you can and teach others to do the same.
- Give your time and talent to non-profit organizations.
- Start your own non-profit organization!

Summation – Impact to Business

As an entrepreneur, you lead your business to create its legacy in the community and be remembered for your community support. To live right and leave a meaningful legacy, you have to invest time in the exploration process. The reflection will help you answer questions about your values, vision, mission, and goals in life. The answers serve as a fertile ground for the seed of your legacy to take root and grow into a solid oak. Living your legacy involves creating strategies to share your values with your loved ones, clients, and the community.

Like business, many families have a family mission statement. Write letters to be shared at special occasions with your loved ones and the community at an interval of one, two, five, and ten years. Leave your loved ones in charge of your foundation to help the community so that not only are you teaching them values while you are alive, but you are engaging them even after your death to uphold your values of giving and helping others.

Legacy Action Exercise
Living Legacy Model – The 1/1/1 Leader Project

This model aims to weave leadership into the very fabric of our community so that it becomes the fiber of our very being; a way of life rather than something we think. We lay the foundation act by act and smile by smile, creating micro-transformations every day.

SIGN The 1/1/1 Leader Project Pledge[8]. The project embraces the simplicity that the modern world has come to embrace. The mission is simple: to create a community of inspired, connected, and supportive individuals. By making the pledge, you are required to complete four simple tasks:

- **SET** Take simple steps towards **one** goal, no matter how simple or complex. Your goal can be as simple as exercising 15 minutes, five times a week or as complex as learning how to become an expert in new software. Write down your goal, and put it in place where you constantly remind yourself of it. Set a period for when you want to accomplish the goal you have set.
- **SMILE** Make someone's day by giving them a smile. That's it, just **one** smile!
- **SERVE** Do **one** good act for someone else. Open a door, compliment them, and get the groceries for someone. Be simple! Everyone tells you to "serve" your community. This will help you.
- **SPREAD** After you've achieved your goal, set another one and continue. Ask one of your friends to sign the pledge.

SHARE Share your success story on our website.

SIMPLE The project prides itself on being simple. Set a goal. Work towards achieving it. Give someone a smile. Be nice to another person. Sign the pledge and make the world a little bit nicer.

Sign. Set. Smile. Serve. Spread. Share. Simple.

1 for yourself. 1 for someone else. 1 for the community.

---

[8]   http://www.divyaparekh.com/111-leader-project/

If you want to sign the pledge, visit at http://www.divyaparekh. com/111-leader-project/

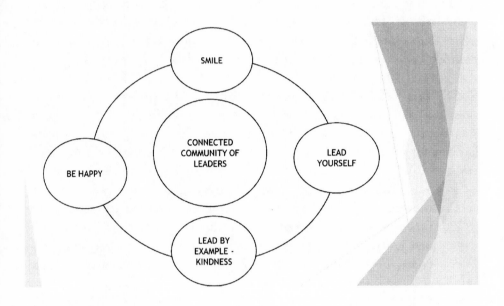

CHAPTER 11

THE RESULTS OF SUCCESS

While it is simple to engage in the discussion of a task, it is not so easy to act on it.
Divya Parekh

Ready to learn about the last relationship, I dialed Dee's number. When she picked up the phone, I cheerfully reminded her, "We have one more relationship to discuss."

Dee laughed at my enthusiasm and said, "Sally, I would love a nice stroll along the beach this Saturday. The weather is supposed to be beautiful. Why don't you come out to the beach house? Meeting on Saturday will give you a few days to contemplate the questions that I will email to you. These will be the last…for now."

Laughing, I replied with a big "Yippee!" Although I enjoyed teasing Dee, her questions were worth books of advice by others. Later in the day, her email came through. I scrolled down and read them:

1. Do you review your business plan quarterly?

2. Is your current business plan reflective of your present purpose/vision, mission, values and goals, deliverables, strategies of execution, and timelines?

3. Are you clear about your overall business plan so that you can communicate it to the team, partners, and relevant parties without any preparation?

4. Have you delivered your business plan in its entirety to your team, partners, and related parties?

5. How do you relate to and overcome your obstacles, challenges, and blind spots?

6. How do you create new opportunities for business, employees, and your customers?

7. Do you have a well-thought-out contingency plan?

Several days later, as we walked barefoot on the beach, I said, "Dee, looking back over our time together, I love how everything you shared with me works so comprehensively in my business and my life. Our conversations have made me think about things in an entirely different way, and I have assimilated the knowledge into what I do. I know my journey wouldn't be so rewarding and stress-free without you being there in my corner."

"Sally, I have so enjoyed being your mentor and coach. To watch you take my concepts and strategies and our jointly designed action plans successfully to the finish line has been incredibly satisfying. I know the process was tough for you at times, but growth happens in discomfort."

Any past pain was far behind me, as though it had occurred in a different lifetime. I yearned to express the value that had resulted from the coaching, and I would have shouted it from the rooftops if I could have. "Having you by my side, looking out for me, and supporting me to maintain a work-life balance took me away from the place I was in when we met. I don't even recognize that person anymore. You helped me identify my blind spots and turn them into assets."

Dee started to say something, but stopped herself, sensing that I wanted to complete my thought. Taking Dee's arm to stop our walk and look her in the eye, I continued, "Dee, I want you to know that as you inspired and cheered me on unfailingly, the integration of relationships in my life empowered me to tackle challenges with a fresh perspective and deal with them to achieve success. At the same time, you taught me to stay aligned with my desires, purpose, and visions. Because of that, I am always looking to make value-based decisions. I am so grateful to you! Not only did this impact me deeply, but I can bring the same knowledge and inspiration to my clients."

I saw that Dee's eyes had teared up a bit, but she quickly overcame it, saying, "It sure beats being an overwhelmed and frustrated entrepreneur. I look at you now and see a confident and humble entrepreneur who is a leader in a wildly successful business."

"Thank you," I said. "Yet, when I looked at your last batch of questions, it made me realize that getting results is great, but I need a continuous improvement plan for continued success."

"You hit the nail on the head, Sally. Until I retired, or whatever you want to call what I do now, I had strong relationships with the two coaches who helped me continue building business momentum and maintain it. Always having a mentor or coach helped me be open-minded, play full out, and achieve success despite obstacles. At the same time, they kept me mindful of aligning my desire, purpose, and vision to make value-based decisions. In return, I did the same for my clients or mentees."

I laughed. "Like you have done for me!"

Dee laughed too and said, "What blew me away was that my coaches had coaches too. I stayed with my coaches because they continued growing as I was growing. When my kids took over the business, and we had created a self-sustaining education and mentoring program, I semi-retired. My coaches and I are friends to this day. I continue volunteering in my businesses and organizations. Of course, I mentor young entrepreneurs like yourself, and I also travel, meditate, and enjoy nature."

"That's what I want in my future," I said. "I did experience a certain contentment after writing down my day-to-day and future legacy plan. While I feel content about my business, I realize there are some gaps. I realize that my environment, my business, and I are consistently changing and evolving. After giving some serious thought to your most recent batch of questions, I realized that implementation requires me to review my short-term and long-term business plans. I have to constantly set new goals and adjust my roadmap accordingly. I understand that we continue to evolve in the plethora of shifting tides."

"That's right, Sally. You will accomplish and surpass your goals as a powerful consequence of successfully balancing all business relationships. The end game is to springboard in becoming a better you with a bigger vision of how you can impact others as you continue to succeed and sustain your success. Once a farmer takes in his harvest, he has the room to think about how he can grow more to feed more. Let's sit on that dune and chat about this relationship. As they say, it is the last, but certainly not the least!"

We left the waterline and sat down. Out came my notebook and phone. As the sun started to fade in the sky, Dee shared with me the last of the relationships.

What is Relationship with Results

Relationship with results matters! Results are the milestones that let us know if we are going in the right direction. Success requires destination and destination needs direction. Life is a journey comprised of many destinations. It is about living a mindful life driven by value-based decisions, learning, unlearning, and relearning while having fun and making life a play. Relationship with results is how you measure success, clearly defining the outcomes, and determining the progress as you work towards your goals.

For example, you define your success criteria by the number of new clients you find. You commit to gaining three new clients in the next three months. If you win those three, you are successful because you have met your goals.

Why Relationship with Results is Important to Business

Starting out with clarity allows you to know who you want to be, where you want to go, and how to get there. Clarity helps you shatter the status quo and step into success by defining your values, vision, mission, goals, and objectives followed by implementing execution strategies, tactics, and tools to achieve your goals. Along the way, you develop great relationships with yourself and other people. As you continue running a successful business, sustainability becomes a major goal in itself. The relationship with results requires the application of the other relationships to garner business success. For sustained success, you ask the following questions:
- Do your business goals support business income and growth?
- What specific and measurable outcomes designate success?

- Do your actual results match desired results?
- What is working well and what could be improved?
- When you do not achieve the set goals, question if the goal changed during the period of execution. Is your planning relevant to the modified goal or do you need to readjust it?

A sapling has to adapt to the changing environment to grow into a healthy tree. For example, it might need more water in the summer and less in the winter. After achieving goals, you need a flexible mindset and strategies to keep your short-term and long-term business plan current, sustainable, and relevant.

The relationship with results enables you to continuously improve all your relationships, systems, processes, products, and services. The efficiency results in business growth as well as cost reduction.

On the other hand, if you increase proficiency in one relationship, then other relationships can lag behind. When that happens, you pay attention to the relationship that has suffered. As a result, sometimes you can undo the efficiencies gained earlier. Thus, you could improve proficiency in one relationship at the expense of others. Quality, cost, delivery, and employee morale usually serve as the measures of performance. There are methods to incorporate in your activities to help your relationship with results.

How to Strengthen the Relationship with Results

Business wisdom demands an in-depth understanding, organization, and management of the nine relationships. Once the company has achieved a level of success, the focus has to be on all relationships to make sound and critical decisions (Action Exercise) for sustained success. There are two key essentials when you analyze your business as a whole and strengthen a relationship without making other aspects suffer.

1. First essential of sustained success – Know the Forest, Know the Trees

- Begin with self-leadership as you lead your team.
- Have a strategy for three, five, and ten years.

- Understand your business from 30,000 feet.
- Understand your business from the trenches by understanding your process.

2. Second essential of sustained success – Continuous Growth and Evolution

- After assessing your results, evaluate your short-term and long-term goals through risk management.
- Create best practices to simplify and improve existing processes and systems, and address your problems.
- Continue the cycle through an adjusted action plan, followed by effective execution and real-time success measurement.

Student Leader for Life – Own Your Learning, Unlearning, and Relearning

As you implement the nine relationships into your life and business, you experience different results. You react or respond to them. As you bring mindfulness to the situation, you make a value-based decision on the results whether it is the desired outcome or not. From there, you decide to continue, improve, or try something else in regards to the result.

You learn that people, strategy, system, and processes work together in synergy. It is important to have a robust, candid dialogue between you, your team, your partners, and your market to gain alignment, create cross-functionality, and determine the realities of business. The culture of your organization should create a safe space for open conversations, questions, and debates that bring the company's real problems to the forefront. When you know the actual problems, you can arrive at practical solutions.

A successful business or organization gets results, celebrates efforts, makes mistakes, and faces failures and challenges. What matters is what you do with each experience. You may experience fear, uncertainty, doubts, criticism from others, etc. Every experience is the fertile ground of growing the seed of learning where you develop best practices from what worked well. You create opportunities for continuous improvement from experiences. If you have a setback, you may need to evaluate and reconsider your strategies. You are grateful for a growth experience.

Meeting milestones lets you know that you are implementing the right strategies. Together, you and your team/partners have created ground rules and benchmarks. Because you have done this process in conjunction with others, the accord between the concerned parties fosters commitment, ownership, and accountability to the project's success.

What you do today will change where your business is tomorrow. You, your team, and partners can:

- Gain clarity concerning vision/purpose, mission, and goals.
- Streamline channels of communication to ensure that there is open communication between the concerned and those individual goals are aligned with organizational goals.
- Join forums, participate in a mastermind group, find an accountability partner, work with a coach, or work it out yourself through books (like this one!).
- Learn, teach, develop and grow yourself, your team/partners, and market.
- Include mindfulness to integrate all relationships with laser focus and unstoppable confidence.

30,000 Feet Business Overview

When your vision/purpose and WHY are clear, you can implement business strategies to integrate systems, adapt processes, and strengthen relationships to attain both short and long term results. That's where the relationships, especially relationships with market, team, and partners established in earlier chapters come into play. It begins with your leadership encompassing every relationship and intersection of relationships in regards to each person's actions. A 30,000foot overview of successful business processes consists of:

- Observing and understanding the connectivity of relationships in an internal and external environment in the business success matrix.

- Assessing every relationship to ensure that short-term and long-term goals are balanced is important.
- Designing short- medium- and long-term critical milestones (business specific measurement metrics) for tracking goal achievement. Ensure that milestones are flexible to account for evolving goals.
- Generating a timeline that accounts for specific, measurable, achievable, relevant, and time-bound goals. Breaking down of goals into manageable tasks makes it easier to accomplish success.
- Understanding that the execution connects dreams and results. A common organizational problem is developing a terrific strategic plan and then ignoring it. In the words of the Nike slogan, "Just do it!"
- Focusing on long-term success involves exploring ideas, innovations, and collaborations as opportunities for continuous improvement, growth, and sustainability.
- Participation of relevant parties in the execution process.
- Celebrating and rewarding yourself and others, when you achieve milestones. Celebrating is important.
- When you fail to reach milestones, learn from it and implement the learning to improve the process. Adjusting the strategies and execution plan based on which relationship needs attention is integral to success. For example, when your team and partners are working great, but your clients are not satisfied with your delivery time, then you pay attention to partners in conjunction with the team to expedite the delivery time to meet your client's needs.
- Assimilating and blending all relationships such that they function as one and work toward the business success as a complete system rather than individual units.

Continuous Growth and Evaluation

Results Assessment

When you start a business, your reference point can be targeted results based on the numbers available from other competitors or current trends. As your business grows, you will collect data over time. At this point, your business data becomes your reference point for generating targeted results. It is essential to evaluate and measure results in real time, identify gaps, and determine if your goals are on track. You can use Excel or sophisticated statistical software to analyze your results. What is vital to success is what you do after you assess your results.

Concurrent Improvement of All Relationships

The secret to the parallel development of all relationships is to eliminate waste or inefficiency in each relationship. For example, when you eliminate overproduction or services that are not generating any income, you reduce business cost. As a side benefit, you improve quality since you can dedicate the time to prevent problems that you might have previously overlooked.

Efficient systems can simplify complex processes, thereby reducing lead times of product or service delivery to the client. As a result, you have happier employees because they feel valued and secure in their job as you invest in systems to make their job easier. As a ripple effect, enthusiastic employees perform at a higher level.

Risk management involves different strategies.

The goal of risk management is to identify risks (consequences), understand them, assess their implications on the business or organization in the future, dissect them, and prioritize them before you take action.

1. First, you define your strategic objectives for one, three, five, and ten years.

2. Then you review last year's performance and the performance trends of the past few years. As you review last year's results, you determine what worked well, what did not work well, and identify risks, potential improvements, and the lessons learned.

3. Assess what you need to do to achieve this year's strategic objectives, what are the benefits of these actions, and if the current year's objectives will form the foundation for long-term objectives.

4. Determine the pros and cons of activities as potential risk through risk assessment. There are several risk assessment tools out there. Select the one that works best for you. When you choose what works best for your company, determine the right people with the experiences for completing it[9].

Summation –The Impact of Results to Business

When you give your blood, sweat, and tears to launch and expand your business, it is important to evaluate every result you have – major or minor, good and bad. You need to approach these results with the same mindfulness you give every other relationship. You can fix the fractured systems and process as well as improve on what is good only through analyzing your results. Maintaining the status quo often leads to stagnation and trouble.

You are the pivot point for your business. You have to own your leadership role. It is your responsibility to stay the course, keep your focus on the short-, mid- and long-term goals, and readjust the course as necessary. Leading yourself with strength and vision while staying aligned to your values will inspire your team and partners to follow your example. When they see you mulling over results, they will do likewise. With so many eyes and ideas involved in the process on this level, your company will effortlessly roll with the punches of any setbacks and grow by leaps and bounds with the successes.

As you lead your business or organization with a mindset of continuous improvement, the quest to evolve leads you to understand results, ensures your planning to stay relevant to goals, and enhances your ability to adjust the course as needed. You accept risks, failures, and successes and evaluate them. This mindset helps you develop resilience and have a perspective that every result is a step to propel you towards your goals.

---

[9] If you want to take the risk assessment one step further, check out success. divyaparekh.com/FMEA for a detailed risk assessment tool.

When you started your business, you began with grit to go after your dreams. During the process, you constantly find yourself stepping out of your comfort zone time and time again. Shattering the discomfort might be difficult for you, but you experience growth and an unstoppable confidence that keeps you on your path while gaining and sustaining momentum. Understanding your results as a consequence of incorporating all the other relationships in your business allows you to continually strengthen and grow your enterprise with a sense of accomplishment, sustainability, and peace.

Results Action Exercise:

A critical decision is one that involves significant outcomes when you face a problem or an opportunity. For instance, identifying your ideal client, deciding on the right financial planner, making the right investments, and many more decisions can have powerful consequences.

For example, you identify your ideal client and then you gear your marketing and products/services to meet their needs. Knowing your market helps you achieve your desired goals. If you don't figure out who your ideal customers are, you keep spinning your wheels trying to figure out why you are not getting enough clients and why people are not responding to your products and services. In either case, the lack of decision or a decision made has a powerful impact on consequences.

Remember to be in a mindful state as you approach any step of decision-making. Mindfulness prevents you from making ineffective decisions under stress or an emotional cloud that could bear negative consequences. If you experience physical or emotional conflicts, work through it with grit and continue forward with the process. As you repeat the process, you will get stronger and stronger and learn to make sound decisions.

How can you make sound and informed critical decisions?

1) Self and Situation Assessment
   - Bring mindfulness to scan your emotions and actions. View the situation from a place of non-judgment.
   - Understand if are you reacting or responding to the problem, issue, or undesirable outcome. Reflect if the problem, issue, or adverse outcome is worth addressing. Reacting can cloud your

judgment where you might become predisposed to blaming the circumstances or people. Responding and owning responsibility for the situation allows you to get to the root cause of the matter on hand.

- Ask questions that will help you to understand the current situation, such as "What caused the problem and who is impacted by it?"
- Review if the problem has occurred before. If it did, was it resolved? Why did it happen again if it was resolved?
- Confirm the root cause with data, evidence, and relevant information.
- Once you know the root cause, it is easier to formulate the decision problem statement.

2) Generate the decision problem statement by:
   - Framing the problem. Is it an opportunity for you, a threat to you, or is there no impact?
   - Asking for team members' or partners' perspectives of the problem to verify that your assessment of the problem is accurate.
   - Revisit the problem statement after one day, two days, and a week. This review allows you to decide if the problem statement needs amending.

3) Define the desired objectives of your decision by asking the following:
   - What would help you clarify your objectives? There is usually a principle behind the need to make a decision. Are you getting the principle across to the decision makers? For example, the principle is that there is a need to increase the revenue before year-end to give bonuses to employees. To do this, you have to decide whether you should do two product launches instead of one without hiring new employees or contractors.
   - Is the objective a must-have or a nice-to-have?
   - How does it impact your business, team members, and partners? Are the right people involved in making the decision?
   - Is the objective aligned with your vision?
   - Does the objective have the potential impact on your future?

4) Generate good alternatives.
   - Look at the problem from different angles and ask yourself how else you can achieve your objectives.
   - Ensure that the assumptions for each alternative are relevant, and you make your decision based on realistic facts, not opinions or biases.
   - Decide if you are utilizing and evaluating the available data, information, and the appropriate resources to come up with alternatives. This process will allow you to go deeper into decision-making as well as make certain that you are making the right choice as you consider different aspects of the problem.

5) Explore alternatives:
   - Examine the risks associated with each alternative solution and assess if they are manageable.
   - Explore the consequences related to each alternative and how the results will impact you and your business in the short-term and long-term.
   - Consider the emotional, customer, financial, cultural, and other relevant benefits of the alternative solutions.

6) Select the best option, make an informed decision, and take action.

7) Prevent the problem from reoccurring by standardizing the work, creating a control plan to minimize the impact of the problem, and train the team in the new solutions.

EPILOGUE

The whole secret of a successful life is to find out what is one's destiny to do, and then do it.

Henry Ford

I helped Dee out of the back of the limo. I wanted this to be a special occasion and spared no expense for the day. When trying to figure out where to hold the celebration, I decided to go back to where it all started for me. That's why we pulled up to Ma Paizen Restaurant. I had reserved their banquet room. Dee thought we were just coming here for dinner.

Wearing a simple black dress with a string of pearls around her neck, she looked 20 years younger than her 85 years. I wore a red dress that I thought of as my party dress. I liked wearing it for special occasions and tonight was one of them.

Once we were inside, I gave a short nod to the party planner who organized this event. Greeting us warmly, she said, "We have a quiet table for you in the back. Please follow me."

I allowed Dee to go first. As we passed through a small archway into another room, about 150 people yelled out, "Surprise!"

Dee spun around to me with a shocked look on her face. I just grinned at her. She looked back around at all of the people who were now gazing at her and applauding. For the first time since I know her, Dee was speechless. Finally, she turned to me with a red blush coloring her cheeks. "I…I don't understand. I don't recognize any of these people."

I waved my hand, and Mikayla and Lynn came over. "Dee," I said, "these are my two best friends I have been telling you about. I have been feeding them all the lessons you taught me. They have embraced them as I have. A year ago, we met in this restaurant lamenting the fact that we felt like our respective businesses were going to bury us. Because of you, we are now thriving. We have expanded our companies and are starting some new ventures. Together we started a nonprofit to help young woman entrepreneurs to get started in business. This dinner is to thank you."

Lynn and Mikayla embraced Dee. They gushed about how her help was so instrumental in their maturation in business. Within minutes, I could see they all made a connection. Wiping a tear from her eye and facing the large crowd who were still applauding, she said, "I appreciate this. Now please tell me about these secret admirers."

Mikayla said, "These are our team members, partners and a good amount of clients. We shared with them how you helped us and how we were throwing this party for you as a way of saying 'Thank you.' Sally has been stressing with us your emphasis on relationships, and also how important it is to celebrate success. We figured we'd combine the two for this evening."

Lynn chimed in. "Dee, you don't realize it, but you have touched all these people in here in some way. There would be more, but this was the largest room we could book on short notice. It doesn't even touch our gratification for the impact you have made on our lives. Now let the party begin – let's have fun!"

The evening flew by. Watching everyone hovering around Dee made it a fun night, and it was clear that my team and partners thoroughly enjoyed themselves. While this event was to honor Dee, I realized that I was further strengthening the bonds with everyone present. I enjoyed watching people getting to know each other and networking. I made a mental note to have more events like this in the future.

When the night was over, I escorted Dee from the car to her home. She said, "Sally, I have had the privilege of mentoring several brilliant people in my life. I am grateful when people really "get" the nine relationships I advocate. I know by your success that you are one of them. What you did tonight for me shows me that you understand the nuances of the relationships. You are going to have a wonderful life."

She took my hand, and we hugged. I whispered the most heartfelt "Thank you" I ever said. She went to her house, and I got back into the car looking forward to tomorrow.

A FINAL WORD

Writing a book is not the solitary experience many people think it is. It is truly an undertaking that reflects the nine relationships I talk about in the book. So many people have influenced my thinking over the years that it is tough to acknowledge everyone. As I sat down to put a list together of the people that supported me to write this book, I found that I was concerned about missing anyone whose valuable input and assistance led to its creation. Since I couldn't bear the thought of accidently doing that, I am sending out a very heartfelt thanks to family, dear friends, partners, clients, and colleagues who were part of the creation process.

I also send out a huge thank you to my long list of advanced readers. It is delightfully humbling to have the help I did. I am forever grateful and appreciative for the time you gave me to review the manuscript and the terrific insights that helped shape the nuances of the story. You all have been in my thoughts during this endeavor.

The core essence of my life's philosophy is to make a huge difference in people's lives. I hope that this book will create a positive impact in your life!

It is my privilege to meet you, and I sincerely hope we can continue the conversation. You can contact me at contact@divyaparekh.com. Please visit my website at www.divyaparekh.com.

WHAT'S NEXT?

Has Sally's journey to becoming a successful entrepreneur sparked something inside of you? Do the interactions and insights Dee and Sally have shared in the book inspire you? If so, THERE IS MORE! Sally is preparing a playbook to supplement the lessons shared in this book during the interlude chapter. She is taking Dee's work on networking and expanding it into a workbook to help you further develop your market, team, and partners.

As The Entrepreneur's Garden – Nine Essential Relationships to Cultivate Your Wildly Successful Business shows the relationships with other people is critical to your growth and success depends on meeting and finding the right people. When you have a neat and orderly garden, the soil yields harvest beyond expectations than if you were to scatter seeds around. Searching for people who will make good partners or members of your team is more productive with a systematic approach. In the playbook, you will reflect on your situation, come up with solutions, and implement them in your life. The playbook will help you plant the seeds you want and reap an abundant harvest. The playbook will illustrate:

- ❖ How to use a step-by-step system to take contacts from connection to collaboration.
- ❖ How to know relationship obstacles and overcome them.
- ❖ The top ten techniques to create rich and meaningful business relationships.
- ❖ How you can mutually support your connections to succeed.
- ❖ How connections can chart the roadmap for your future.

If you are interested in being one of the first ones to get the playbook, reach out to me at contact@divyaparekh.com

Committed to your success,

Divya

Copyright Notice

CPSIA information can be obtained
at www.ICGtesting.com
Printed in the USA
FSOW01n1351221116
27717FS